AMERICAN GARDENING SERIES

DRIED FLOWERS

Martha E. Kraska

MACMILLAN • USA

My thanks to Suzanne F. Bales, Kay Macy, Betty Decker, and Gina Norgard

MACMILLAN
A Prentice Hall Macmillan Company
15 Columbus Circle
New York, New York 10023

Library of Congress Cataloging-in-Publication Data

Kraska, Martha.
Dried flowers / Martha E. Kraska.
p. cm.—(Burpee American gardening series)
Includes index.
ISBN 0-671-85041-5
1. Dried flowers. 2. Flower gardening. 3. Dried flowers—Pictorial works. I. Title. II. Series.
SB428.5.K73 1995
635.9'73—dc20 94-5204
CIP

PHOTOGRAPHY CREDITS
Agricultural Research Service
Bales, Suzanne Frutig
Horticultural Photography, Corvallis, OR
Kraska, Martha
Lindtner, Peter
Royal Sluis
Sluis Groot
W. Atlee Burpee & Co.

Designed by Levavi & Levavi

Manufactured in the United States of America

10 9 8 7 6 5 4 3 2 1

On the cover: Limonium sinuatum.
Preceding page: *A collection of flowers and seed heads for drying.*

CONTENTS

INTRODUCTION

At the end of the winter I look forward to the awakening of the garden. I delight in the first signs of spring and the sight of each and every bulb, tree, shrub and flower. I eagerly anticipate the gathering of the first of many floral bouquets. However, this yearly ritual brings mixed feelings because in the best of circumstances, the cut flowers will last only a few days in water. If only they could last longer! Since the beginning of time, people have wished to preserve the beauty of nature throughout the long winter months.

In my quest to learn more about preserving flowers, I have met many people who have taken on the hobby of flower drying and who treat it as an art, sometimes devoting their full time to it. Most of the enthusiasts plant, grow, nurture, harvest and dry their own flowers and ultimately create wonderful displays.

It is estimated that 80 percent of flowers can be successfully dried and preserved. This was a surprise to me because I had always thought of dried flowers as everlastings. The term *everlasting* brings to mind an arrangement of lifeless flowers in a limited range of beige, yellow and orange colors.

I started to look at the other flowers in the garden, wondering about their drying potential, and began to experiment. I now realize that everlastings are just a small portion of the possible flowers and shrubs for air-drying and preserving. The range of flowers that I dry has grown along with the size of my garden. I'm always learning of new flowers to dry and have begun to exchange with friends the seed of many new and unusual flowers suitable for drying. Experimentation is a big part of the process. When you start out, try your hand at drying any plant material that appeals to you. The plant world is full of materials that make interesting additions to dried flower arrangements. Various foliage, branches of trees and shrubs, pinecones, nuts, gourds, grasses and even mosses contribute interest to your displays.

Many of the flowers I thought were too difficult for a novice to dry are now my favorites. Rosebuds, which are so expensive to purchase dried, can be easily air-dried from your own rosebushes. Cut the roses in the bud stage and hang them to air-dry. What could be easier? Peonies can be dried in the same way. They will fade in color and shrink a bit in size but you will still be delighted with their crepe-paper appearance. Every garden holds its own pleasant surprises. If you garden at all, you already have many wonderful flowers for drying. Many common perennials are easy to dry. Some herbs have tiny flowers that dry easily, while others provide the beauty of their aromatic foliage. For a bonus, tuck these fragrant herbs into your dried bouquets and arrangements.

In your search for new and different materials, don't forget to search your roadsides and fields. Nature provides a wealth of plant materials to be used in dried arrangements and bouquets. You will be delighted with many of the roadside treasures. (When collecting in the wild, remember that you should never deplete the roadside flowers. Leave at least a dozen behind, and use care not to disturb the roots. This way you will ensure their future beauty.)

Every season holds its own special dried treats. After the flowers fade, many plants retain seedpods and seed heads that are unusual, interesting and beautiful in arrangements.

The art of flower drying has advanced rapidly over this century and there are new techniques to help retain the lasting beauty of flowers. I suggest you start with the simplest technique—air-drying. Once you have mastered air-drying, you may decide to try your hand at more involved drying techniques. Using these methods, you can produce a dried flower that looks as fresh as the day it was picked.

A small wreath of dried flowers surrounds the base of this charming antique lamp.

1

THE DRIED FLOWER GARDEN PLANNER

DRIED FLOWER GARDEN DESIGN

When I first started drying flowers, I grew only everlasting annuals in a cutting garden. Everlastings are flowers that, when dry, naturally retain their color and shape for many years. I gave no thought to the design or color of the garden when planting them because they were only grown to be harvested and used in dried arrangements and crafts. Many of these everlastings were beautiful and worthy of a better home (perhaps in one of the more formal perennial or annual display gardens, tubs, pots or window boxes), but I grew them in tidy rows until they were harvested for dried arrangements. Today I look at the same flowers in a very different way. Not only do I use them throughout the garden, but I have come to appreciate their true value as sturdy, long-blooming and highly decorative flowers. Now I love to use them in containers and window boxes, where they can grow until the arrival of a killing frost. These easy-going flowers can also withstand the heat and dryness of such confined spaces.

Not all flowers for drying are everlasting; many annuals, perennials and shrubs can be easily preserved. Take a walk in your garden and I am sure you will find a bounty of materials just waiting to be harvested for drying. Many popular garden plants, such as peonies, roses and hydrangeas, are candidates for drying, and you might already have some growing in your garden.

If you decide to grow flowers specifically for drying, you will need to choose the plants and the type of garden that will suit your needs best. Those people lucky enough to have lots of space may want to create a separate cutting garden of dried and everlasting flowers. In this kind of cutting garden, annual flowers are grown in tidy rows without regard to color, height or bloom time. Cutting gardens are simple, yet highly productive. If, however, you have limited space but would love to grow dried and everlasting flowers, try mixing them into your existing annual and perennial borders.

THINK ANNUALS

Annuals are plants that complete their life cycles in one growing season. One of the great features of annuals is that they can be harvested and enjoyed in just a few weeks. Annuals come in a wide range of colors, textures and heights, and most are easy to grow from seed. Everlastings are annual flowers with petals that are naturally strawlike and stiff, even when growing. You will find that everlastings can be very useful in the garden because they hold their color throughout the summer and tolerate heat and dryness. They can also be harvested in stages to prevent bare spots in midsummer. Some of the more unusual everlastings are *Lunaria annua* (money plant), *Moluccella laevis* (bells of Ireland) and *Lagurus ovatus* (hare's-tail grass).

Many flowers for drying can be collected in fields and meadows. Here Queen Anne's lace and goldenrod fill an old basket.

Because many annuals like cooler weather, you can get a jump on sowing their seeds. For example, larkspur, bachelor's buttons, Iceland poppies and nigella all prefer direct sowing in early spring or late winter. Try sowing the seeds of these plants in late autumn in colder areas, because they will begin their growth in the cooler temperatures of early spring. Most annuals are sown after danger of frost in the spring. (In warmer southern climates they can be sown in fall.) See the plant portrait section for individual plant needs.

If you don't want to grow your own annuals from seed, you can purchase flats of seedlings ready to pop into the garden from many garden centers. Most garden centers, however, don't carry the more unusual annual varieties. If you are looking for some different annuals, you will probably need to sow your own seed. Try some of the many specialty catalogs that cater to the dried-flower lover, or collect and save your favorite seeds to use the next year. Some annuals have the habit of self-sowing and will return to the garden year after year. These self-sowers are easy to eradicate if unwanted but, if left to grow, will add a charm and softness to any garden.

Some of my favorite annuals for drying are marigolds, zinnias, celosia and ageratum. I also adore salvias. Annual and biennial salvias are easy to grow, and they bring an unmatched beauty both to the garden and to dried arrangements. The biennial *Salvia sclarea* (clary sage) is a real eye-catcher in the garden border. It has striking, whitish-blue flowers with white- and rose-colored bracts. Another terrific salvia for drying is *Salvia viridis* (also known as *S. horminum*), which produces multicolored flowers of white, pink, blue and purple all on the same stem. 'Indigo Spires', a majestic 5-foot-tall salvia, has intense purple-blue spikes that appear in late summer.

A cutting garden of drying flowers would not be complete without an assortment of gomphrena.

Try growing your everlasting in a showy display garden, like this one of celosia, statice, nigella, and strawflower.

Above, left;
Many perennials dry easily. Here a border containing yarrow, ornamental grasses, salvias, and ornamental alliums are all perfect for dried arrangements.

Above, right;
Don't overlook many of your popular perennials such as hydrangea, coneflower, salvia, and nepeta. They are all easy to dry.

LOOK TO YOUR PERENNIAL BORDERS

Your perennial garden is another source of wonderful dried flowers. A perennial is any plant that dies down every winter and returns the following season. Many perennials are both easy to grow and easy to dry. Some of the best perennials for drying are also frequent components of perennial garden designs. Flowers such as yarrow (*Achillea millefolium*), pearly everlasting (*Anaphalis*), wormwood (*Artemisia*), goldenrod (*Solidago canadensis*) and feverfew (*Chrysanthemum parthenium*) dry easily and are common enough that you may already be growing them. Catnip (*Nepeta*), the friend of the feline, is also the friend of the dried-flower enthusiast. It is a sturdy perennial with attractive, long-blooming blue flowers on gracefully arched stems. Air-drying retains its fresh, minty fragrance. Catnip combines with coralbells for a striking combination of color and texture. Another wonderful combination is the majestic *Echinacea* (coneflower), planted alongside *Echinops* (the globe thistle). They are tolerant of dry, hot conditions, and the warm pink of *Echinacea* and the steel blue of *Echinops* prove a striking combination both in the garden and in dried arrangements. The late-blooming *Sedum* 'Autumn Joy' is always a wonderful sight. Try combining it with the silvery foliage of lamb's ear for a winning combination both in the garden and in your dried arrangements. Don't overlook some of the wonderful filler materials such as *Gypsophila paniculata* (baby's breath), and perennial grasses such as *Miscanthus sinensis*, which produces wonderful pale beige wisps.

In most cases, if growing perennials from seed, you will have to wait until the second growing season for blooms. A garden of perennials will take several seasons to fill in and become established, but the results are well worth the wait. Most perennials have a bloom period of several weeks. And if you select them properly, your garden can be in bloom from earliest spring well into fall.

Foliage

Green is a restful color ever-present in nature. Plants such as ferns, inkberry and boxwood hold their green color even when dry. Green foliage will help create a more natural-looking arrangement. Many of the green foliage materials can be dried using glycerine (see page 26) or by pressing (see page 27). Not all foliage will remain green after drying; some will turn a bronze color. Use the bronze foliage materials to add a warm look to your arrangements. Another important foliage color is silver. Many of my favorite foliage plants, such as artemisia and dusty miller, provide a perfect neutral color to use as a background material.

This cottage garden contains many beautiful dahlias, which when dried in silica gel retain much of their natural color and shape.

Many popular garden flowers can be successfully preserved.

COLOR

Color is one of the most essential elements in designing your garden. If you grow flowers of complementary colors, your dried flower arranging will be made easy. Many of the everlasting flowers (gomphrena, for example) have strong colors that need careful placement in the borders. *Gomphrena* 'Buddy', a lively royal purple flower, looks terrific when grown next to shades of pink, white or even the sunny yellow of coreopsis. Vibrant colors such as yellow and orange will bring warmth and excitement to your arrangements. Strong colors are certainly important in the garden and in dried arrangements.

But remember that white is also indispensable; it helps to create harmony among the other colors. The white *Ammobium* (winged everlasting) and *Anaphalis* (pearly everlasting), for example, complement the strong rose and crimson colors of *Aster novae-belgii.* White also brightens up both the garden and arrangements. You'll find that pink roses are beautiful in combination with the blue of lavender. Experiment with color combinations to find your favorites!

Hydrangeas and other flowering shrubs provide a range of colors as they mature. If you harvest hydrangea flowers throughout their growing cycle, you will have many different shades of flowers, from deep blue to pale pink. Flowers that are allowed to dry on the bush will turn a showy, silvery-beige color. Be sure to check your garden often for subtle color changes in flowers and other plants.

Filler Plants

You have probably found that filler and background materials such as baby's breath, sea lavender, sweet Annie, German statice and various ornamental grasses are important additions to your garden. They are valuable in your dried arrangements, where they create a full, lush look. These airy plants provide soft flowing shape to your arrangements.

A striking combination of lythrum and purple loose strife planted behind Artemisia ludoviciana *'Silver King'.*

MIXED BORDER

The real advantage of a mixed border for the flower drier is that it provides a broader array of plants for drying. When planning your garden for dried material, don't overlook shrubs, trees and vines. Mixing perennials, annuals, herbs, shrubs, roses, bulbs and vines into one garden spot has been a common practice in England for hundreds of years. However, this concept is new to Americans—we tend to separate annuals, perennials and shrubs into their own borders. Combining many types of plants will give you a longer display of color and interest and a more exciting garden.

Shrubs are important additions to the landscape and to the mixed border. Many produce showy flower heads, berries or seedpods that both enhance the garden and also dry beautifully. Several different shrubs for drying are listed on page 14. They range in height from 2 feet to taller varieties, such as lilac, that will reach 20 feet.

Herbs can add interest, beauty and fragrance to your summer flower borders. Fragrant herbs such as sage, mint and rue retain much of their fragrance when dried. Use them in potpourri or press them dry. Most herbs are extremely sturdy and can withstand heat, drought and poor soil. The following herbs produce attractive flowers and air-dry easily: *Origanum* (oregano), which has tiny pink clusters of flowers; *Tanacetum* (tansy), with sunny yellow, buttonlike flowers; and *Anethum graveolens* (dill), with delicate, lacy flower heads. Plant *Calamintha nepetoides,* a pretty thymelike plant, alongside your pathways, in order to enjoy its fragrance and beauty during the summer and to collect for drying at the end of the season.

Trees are not normally thought of as material for drying. However, many flowering trees have decorative flowers, foliage and berries that can be dried. Dogwood, for example, is a prime candidate for dried material. Its foliage keeps a lovely green color when dried in silica gel. And when air-dried, the flowers have a ribbon-like appearance. Colorful fall leaves such as those of the Japanese red maple can be preserved in glycerin. Glycerin helps leaves hold their lovely color. So be sure to look up as well as down when checking the garden for drying possibilities.

Roadside flowers. Queen Anne's lace and black-eyed Susans are perfect additions to informaldried arrangements.

SHRUBS FOR DRYING

Latin Name	**Common Name**
Buxus	boxwood, English form
Callicarpa	beauty-berry
Caryopteris	blue mist spirea
Deutzia	slender deutzia
Hydrangea	hydrangea
Ilex glabra	inkberry
Leucothoe fountaniesiana	leucothoe
Salix	pussy willow
Syringa	French lilac
Viburnum carlesii	viburnum
V. marieseii	
V. plicatum	
Vitex Agnus-castus	chaste tree

TREES FOR DRYING

Acer argutum	Japanese maple
Cornus	dogwood
Eucalyptus	sweet gum
Liriodendron tulipifera	tulip tree

VINES FOR DRYING

Akebia	five-leaf akebia
Celastrus	bittersweet
Clematis spp.	clematis
Wisteria	wisteria

HERBS FOR DRYING

(See page 24 for extensive list of herbs to air-dry.)

Allium schoenoprasum	chive
Anethum graveolens	dill
Origanum	oregano
Tanacetum	tansy

ROADSIDE FINDS

Many wildflowers that bloom in open meadows and alongside busy highways dry easily and add a certain informal charm to your arrangements. Most of these plants are best left growing in the wild because they tend to be invasive in a garden. Planting them in the garden can mean hours of removal and their certain return the following year. Queen Anne's lace is one such plant better left along the road. While its lovely, lacy flowers are unmatched for their delicate beauty, it is considered a weed by most gardeners. *Solidago* (goldenrod) is another invasive wildflower, but its showy, tall, yellow flowers dry beautifully. If you know that a plant is considered a weed or is in tremendous abundance such as Queen Anne's lace, collect some, but not all, of the flowers. Allow a good number of flowers to remain to reseed for next season. Carefully cut the flower heads of perennials, using caution not to disturb the roots.

ROADSIDE PLANTS FOR DRYING

Latin Name	**Common Name**
Aruncus dioicus	goat's beard
Clematis paniculata	Sweet autumn clematis
Eurpatorium purpureum	Joe Pye weed
Rudbeckia hirta	black-eyed Susan
Rudbeckia purpurea	cone flowers
Solidago	goldenrod
Typha latifolia	cattail

SEED HEADS

Seed heads or pods often surpass the beauty of the flowers themselves. Poppies, for example, are truly beautiful when in bloom, and then they develop a wonderful seed head just as lovely. Allow seed heads to remain on stalks to provide an interesting autumn display. Harvest and hang, or stand to air-dry in late autumn.

PLANTS WITH INTERESTING SEED HEADS

Latin Name	**Common Name**
Acanthus mollis	bear's-beech
Allium	ornamental and edible onion
Aquilegia	columbine
Centaurea macrocephala	globe centaurea
Cynara cardunculus	cardoon
Iris foetidissima	gladwin iris
Nigella damascena	love-in-a-mist
Papaver somniferum	opium poppy
Physalis alkekengi	Chinese lantern
Sedum spectabile	sedum

Allium seed pod

Don't be too quick to deadhead! Many flowers produce interesting and attractive seed heads.

2

DRIED FLOWER PLANTING AND GROWING GUIDE

PREPARING THE GARDEN SITE

Preparing your garden site properly is the key to successful gardening. If you provide good drainage and soil that is loose and free of weeds, your plants will flourish. A garden that is properly prepared will produce more flowers. It will also give plants the strength to fight insects and disease.

After you have chosen your garden site, determine the size and shape of the garden. Remove anything that is growing on your chosen site, being especially thorough in pulling up weeds. Add the grass or weeds you have removed to the compost heap or mulch pile. Next, spade or rototill the soil to the depth of 18 inches, incorporating compost or peat moss, topsoil, lime and well-rotted manure. Work all of these ingredients together as if you were mixing a cake batter. If you are preparing the site in early spring, allow a week for the area to settle before planting.

Autumn is the perfect time to prepare any new site because all of the ingredients will mix and settle over the winter months, which allows for an early start to planting in the spring. Autumn is also an excellent time to have the soil tested. A soil test will give you a reading of the acidity or alkalinity of your soil. This is a pH reading, on a scale from 0 to 14, 7 being neutral. Most annuals thrive in a soil that is 6.5 to 7.0 percent. Adding compost, and mulches such as pine needles, will cause some fluctuation in acidity. This relatively inexpensive test will save money in lost plants because it will tell exactly what you need to add to your soil to prepare it for a good growing season. Many garden centers will test your soil and help you select the correct soil amendments. You can also send a soil sample to your local Agriculture Extension Service. They will send you a soil reading along with complete instructions on what is needed to bring your soil to the ideal pH. Most soils are already slightly acid, which is good for growing many of the plants for drying.

To learn what type of soil you have, take a handful of wet soil and squeeze it. If it forms a ball and holds together well, you have clay. If it sifts through your fingers, it is sand. If, however, it holds together showing the imprint of your fingers, and then slowly crumbles as you release it, your soil is loam. Although different plants thrive in different types of soil, loam is possibly the best all-around soil for your garden.

Drainage is an important part of soil preparation. Many dried flowers will not tolerate the wet feet caused by slow-draining soils. Without proper drainage, all of your hard work is futile. Poor drainage also means poor root development. Roots sitting in water and deprived of air have stunted growth, which leads to certain disaster. To check for proper drainage, dig a hole 12 inches deep. Fill the hole with water and allow the water to settle overnight. If water remains in the hole after 24 hours, you have a problem. Fortunately, most drainage problems can be corrected. A major cause of drainage problems is heavy clay soil. Adding sand, organic matter and other porous material such as

Celosia comes in an array of colors from soft yellow to brilliant red.

Clay soil

Sandy soil

Loamy soil

gypsum to your soil should help correct this problem. If the situation is serious, you may need to install drainage pipes under or around the garden site. You can also try using raised beds, which allow excess water to drain below the root level of the plants.

COMPOSTING

Compost, or "black gold" as it is often called, is the end product of broken-down kitchen waste, leaves and other organic matter. A finished compost pile produces dark, nutritious humus that will improve the texture of your garden soil. Creating a compost pile is as easy as choosing an out-of-the-way spot to deposit all leaves, grass clippings and other biodegradable materials. Simply add to the pile and allow it to break down over time. Add a generous layer of compost onto the garden surface before planting time or in early spring before perennials begin to grow.

Compost Bin Design

Most gardeners find it neater to contain their compost pile. Your compost container can be as simple as a circle of wire mesh, about 4 feet high, wrapped around four solid stakes set in the ground deep enough to provide permanent support. Or, you can set concrete blocks as three sides of a rectangle, leaving the fourth side open to allow you access to the finished compost. Finally, plastic compost bins are available from garden catalogs and garden stores; they do an excellent job and look neat in a corner of the garden.

Speeding Up the Compost

Dead leaves, grass clippings that have not been treated with weed killer, weeds that have not gone to seed and vegetable matter such as peelings of fruit and vegetables make excellent compost, as do tea leaves and coffee grounds. Some gardeners recommend that you layer the compost ingredients to speed up the process. Start your compost pile on a layer of twigs or small branches or on cinder blocks, to allow good air circulation. When you achieve about a 6-inch layer of compost, dust the top with lime and add an inch of garden soil. Repeat these layers and keep the pile moist, but not soaked. You don't want to drown the bacteria that decompose the compost materials for you. While the bacteria work they heat the pile, which also helps speed decomposition. Every so often, turn the pile so the material around the edges moves to the inside area where the work of breaking down the ingredients takes place.

PLANTING YOUR GARDEN

After you have prepared your soil, it is time to place your plants. Depending on the size of your garden, you may want to draw a diagram on paper first, showing the position of the plants. If your garden is small you may decide simply to place the pots onto the garden site and move them about until you are pleased with the results. Most perennials need at least 18 inches between each plant, while annuals can be planted from 8 to 10 inches apart. Planting odd numbers (three or five) of each plant assures a more natural look in the garden design.

The ideal time to plant your garden is after the last frost in spring or in early autumn, when the temperatures are cooler and the days shorter. It is better to plant on an overcast day or in the late afternoon to avoid stressing the tender new plants. If you must plant on a hot, sunny day, remember to cover the plants during the heat of the day with a sun screen or makeshift tent of newspapers or cardboard.

Once your plants are in their new home, they will need a drink. Water them close to their base and avoid using a heavy spray. They will need frequent and generous drinks of water in their first few weeks in the garden. When planting shrubs or larger plants, scoop a small indentation around the base of the plant to act as a saucer to hold the water close to the roots, where it is most needed. Planting time is the perfect time to install a soaker hose to remain in the garden during the growing season. Carefully place the soaker hose evenly through the garden, burying it about halfway into the soil. When the plants fill in and mulch is added, the hose will not be noticeable. Soaker hoses are most effective and use far less water than other means of watering. If you don't have one, use any sprinkler with a gentle spray that thoroughly soaks the garden. The best way to check for proper wetness is to dig into the garden in several spots. The soil should be moist at least 1 inch deep.

Once your garden is started, you will face the age-old problem of keeping the weeds in check. You will find that the less space between plants, and the faster the plants grow together, the fewer weeds you will have. In my perennial garden, quite old and lush with plants, the weeds have little room to develop. However, my annual gardens keep me very busy indeed if not mulched early in the growing season.

A good organic mulch is the best way to control the weeds that will undoubtedly attack your garden. Remember to spread several layers of mulch on the garden as soon as possible after planting. It will block out much of the sunlight, and this helps prevents weed seeds from germinating in the soil. There are many kinds of mulch, including shredded bark, pine needles and cocoa or buckwheat hulls, to name a few. Mulches are available at local garden centers (but this can become quite costly, depending on the size of your garden). You can also make your own mulch from shredded grass clippings or layered newspapers. Place several pages of newspaper on the ground and cut planting holes through the paper. While not attractive, this method is inexpensive and effective. Take my word for it, mulch is essential to controlling weeds and will save time and work later.

Gomphrena *'Lavender Queen' is a must for dried flower arrangements.*

STARTING SEED INDOORS

Many of the everlasting annual flowers take three months or more to flower when grown from seed. You can give them a jumpstart by planting them indoors in late winter. In my Zone 7 area I begin about February. Growing from seed is a time-consuming, yet truly rewarding, process. You must follow some simple steps to assure your success. Start by purchasing a good sterile potting medium. This potting medium must be throughly moist, but not soaking wet. Place it in potting trays or individual plastic pots. Next, check your seed packages for the needs of the individual seed. Some larger seeds must be nicked or soaked before planting. Most of the larger seeds will need to be covered with about ¼ inch of the medium. However, some require light to germinate and need nothing but a gentle tamping onto the medium surface. After you have planted according to the packet directions, spritz lightly with water and cover the tray or flat with a large plastic bag or plastic dome cover. To hasten germination, place the flat on top of the refrigerator or on any warm, but not hot, surface. I use a heating blanket for this purpose. Heating blankets can be purchased through catalogs and garden centers. They provide the proper bottom heat and speed germination considerably. Remember to check your flats daily for signs of germination and to make sure the medium is moist. As soon as germination takes place, move the flats from the heating blanket to a sunny window or under grow lights. Place seedlings 2 to 3 inches below the lights; placing seedlings farther away from the lights will cause them to reach toward the light and become scraggly. Thin the plants to allow proper root development. The best way to thin tiny seedlings and not harm their tender roots is to cut them out with a sharp pair of small scissors. Check seed packages for individual needs.

When the temperature outdoors warms up, you should start to harden your seedlings off. Hardening off protects the tender seedlings while allowing them to adjust to the outdoor environment. To harden off, place the seedlings in a protected outdoor spot without too much direct sunlight. Cover them or take them inside every evening to protect them from cooler evening temperatures. In about one week the seedlings should be fully hardened off and ready to plant outside.

Annual Salvia horminum *'Pink Sundry'*

3

METHODS FOR DRYING FLOWERS

DRIED FLOWERS . . . ALL DRIED UP

In earlier, more romantic days, a single flower was placed between the pages of a book or bible to preserve its beauty. Even scientists used heavy books to carry home new and unusual plant material for study. Drying methods have since become more advanced, and today we have a variety of ways to preserve flowers and retain much of their natural beauty. The six basic methods of preserving flowers and foliage are air-drying, water-drying, drying in a microwave oven, using desiccants, preserving in glycerine, and pressing. Each method has its advantages and its disadvantages and some methods are better for some plants than for others. For example, foliage dries best if preserved in glycerine. Air-drying is the simplest method. And when the dessication method is used, flowers retain their natural color and shape (indeed, they're often mistaken for fresh flowers). Serious flower driers use all the basic methods, alone and in combination.

For success with all methods of drying flowers, remember a few simple steps when harvesting. Pick flowers at the correct time in their development—before the color has faded and the petals begin to drop. Harvest in midmorning, after the night's dew has dried and before the heat of midday has caused the flowers to wilt. Check the flowers to make sure they are free of insect damage and discoloration. The smallest imperfection will be magnified after the drying process. Remove thorns from flowers (roses in particular) before drying. They will only become more difficult to handle safely after they are dried.

Whichever drying technique you use, the faster the moisture is removed from the plants, the better they will hold their true color and shape. However, do not rush the process by placing the material too close to a furnace or oven. Heat will make your flowers look faded and they will become brittle and too delicate to handle. The length of time needed to dry flowers varies depending on the amount of moisture in the drying room and the size and denseness of the individual flower. Under the right conditions, most flowers and foliage will take from two to four weeks to dry. Once dry, they can remain in the drying room until needed.

AIR-DRYING

Air-drying is one of the oldest and easiest methods of flower drying. Elaborate equipment is unnecessary; however, a dehumidifier is important if you live in an extremely humid region. To air-dry, flowers can be hung upside down, placed on a drying rack or kept in an upright position. While air-dried flowers will never have the same intensity of color that fresh flowers have, they will lend a charm of their own to dried bouquets and other projects. Some dried flowers—the everlastings in particular—remain close to their original colors; others fade considerably. Blue and yellow retain their original intensity, and red deepens, often becoming brownish. Soft colors such as pale pink and white usually fade into an antique creamy color.

Top: An unused coat closet can be easily turned into a drying room.

Many flowers air-dry well when hung in a warm, dry place for several days.

Flowers often shrink in size after drying. Peonies and roses, for example, shrink considerably but are still lovely additions to arrangements.

Most flowers need a minimum of preparation before air-drying. However, those with weak stems and heavy flower heads (such as roses, peonies, dahlias and strawflowers) will need wiring before drying. Clip the stems to about ½ inch from the flower and gently feed a length of 21-gauge florist wire up the stem and into the head of the flower. Hide the wire by wrapping it with green floral tape or another stem. Make sure the wire is not sticking out of the flower's center; this will become more noticeable and unattractive as the flower dries.

Most air-dried flowers are hung upside down in bunches because the weight of the flower heads causes the stems to dry straight. Group together small bunches of spiky flowers, such as lavender or blue salvia, wrap with a rubber band, and hang to dry. The rubber band will tighten as the material begins to dry and shrink, which prevents the flowers from slipping out. Hang large, double flowers individually to make sure the blooms are not crushed. The bunches and individual flowers can be hung from a hook, wooden rod, rack, coat hanger or any other sturdy support.

Seed heads and pods, rosebuds, larkspur and double hollyhocks will dry best if placed horizontally on a drying rack, screen or any open airy surface that allows air circulation. Flowers with heavy flower heads, such as peonies, dry best when supported by a wire rack in an upright position. To do this, fit a piece of chicken wire over the mouth of a container to hold the stems apart. Flowers and grasses that have been air-dried in an upright position will have more naturally curved stems.

After drying, continue to protect the flowers from their two biggest enemies—moisture and direct sunlight. To control excessive moisture, it is often necessary to purchase a dehumidifier.

Marigolds are secured in bunches and hooked over a wire clothes hanger for drying.

Large, open flowers, such as peonies, are best dried horizontally on wire racks.

FLOWERS FOR AIR-DRYING

Latin Name	Common Name
Achillea	yarrow
Ageratum	ageratum
Alchemilla spp.	lady's mantle
Allium spp.	onions, garlic, chives
Artemisia ludovicianaalbula	artemisia 'Silver King'
A. stellerana	dusty miller
Buxus sempervirens	box, common
Centaurea cyanus	cornflower, bachelor's button
Chrysanthemum spp. and varieties	chrysanthemum
Daucus carota	Queen Anne's lace
Humulus lupulus	hop, common
Hydrangea macrophylla	hydrangea
H. paniculata	hydrangea
Lavandula spp.	lavender
Paeonia spp.	peony
Rudbeckia spp.	coneflower
Salvia farinacea	sage, blue
S. sclarea	clary sage
Santolina	lavender cotton
Solidago spp.	goldenrod
Stachys byzantina	lamb's ears
Tanacetum vulgare	tansy, common
Zinnia	zinnia

BERRIES AND SEEDPODS TO AIR-DRY

Latin Name	Common Name
Callicarpus	beauty-berry
Celastraceae	bittersweet
Lunaria annua	honesty
Nigella	love-in-a-mist
Papaver	Oriental poppy
Physalis alkekengi	Chinese lantern
Rosa	rose (hips)
Rudbeckia hirta	black-eyed Susan

HERBS FOR AIR-DRYING

Latin Name	Common Name
Allium	garlic and chive (flowers)
Anethum	dill (seed heads)
Artemisia	wormwood, southernwood, tarragon
Hyssopus officinalis	hyssop (blooms)
Foeniculum vulgare	fennel (seed heads)
Laurus	bay (foliage)
Lavandula	lavender (blooms)
Mentha	mints (foliage, blooms)
Nepeta	catnip (blooms)
Ocimum	basil (blooms)
Origanum	oregano (foliage, blooms)
Pelargonium	geraniums, scented (foliage)
Rosemarinus officinalis	rosemary (foliage, blooms)
Stachys	lamb's ear (blooms, foliage)

For Success with Air-Drying

Keep your humidity under 50 percent
Provide good air circulation
Avoid overcrowding to retain natural shapes
Provide a warm spot but avoid high heat, which causes excessive dryness
Check flowers for signs of insects or insect eggs before hanging to air-dry
Store dried flowers in a moisture-free area after drying
Spray finished arrangements with a dried flower preservative

WATER-DRYING

Many plants retain their natural color and shape when dried standing in a small amount of water. This method sounds counterintuitive, but it is one of the best ways to dry flowers such as hydrangeas. To water-dry flowers, stand them upright (through chicken wire) with the bottom of their stems in 2 inches of water. Place in a warm, dark and airy room, away from harsh sunlight, and let the water evaporate.

FLOWERS TO WATER-DRY

Latin Name	Common Name
Achillea filipendulina	fernleaf yarrow
Celosia cristata	cockscomb
Gypsophila paniculata	baby's breath
Hydrangea paniculata arborescens	hydrangea 'Grandiflora'
Moluccella laevis	bells-of-Ireland

This wreath of dried flowers will remain beautiful for many months.

DESICCATION

Desiccants are powdery materials that absorb moisture. For many centuries, certain household products such as borax, cornmeal and sand were used effectively as desiccants. These products all act in much the same way: They draw out the moisture from the petals while leaving the flower intact. Unfortunately, they take a very long time to dry, and the result is faded and lifeless blossoms. In recent years, silica gel, which is sold under several different trade names, has been developed for flower drying. Although the name *silica gel* makes me think of a gelatin-style substance, it is actually granular. It is quite similar to fine sugar in texture. It dries flowers quickly and leaves them with their natural vibrant colors and attractive shape. Silica gel is the best method to use when drying flowers that are too delicate or large to air-dry. One of the disadvantages of using silica gel is its initial expense. However, you can effectively reactivate it after several uses by heating it in a low oven to remove the moisture it has absorbed from the flowers.

You can dry countless kinds of flowers using the silica gel method. A few flowers that are good to start with are pansies, roses and daisies. Prepare the flowers by clipping the stems about ½ inch from the flower heads. Longer stems make laying the flower heads in the container difficult. Gently feed thin-gauge floral wire into the cut stem, and carefully press it through the flower center. Bend the wire to the side, which will allow the flower heads to lay flat in the container. Flowers with a single layer of petals (such as daisies, dianthus and violets) should be dried face down in the drying medium with their stems sticking out of the material. Before placing the flowers into the container, build tiny mounds of silica gel on which to rest the individual flower heads. Then cover the entire underside of the flower head with silica gel. When drying flowers with double petals, place them face up on a 2-inch layer of silica gel. Pour the gel around the outside petals of the flower head carefully. Continue to pour the silica gel into every part of the flower head, taking care to keep its natural shape. The size and shape of the flower you wish to dry will dictate the size and height of the container you use. All containers must be airtight. To further control the moisture, try using a dehumidifier in the drying room.

The more flowers you dry, the more you will learn their individual needs. For example, the trick for keeping the natural closed petal shape of a tulip is to place it in a paper cup with its stem through a hole in the cup's bottom. The cup will support the petals and keep them closed. Gently pour the silica gel into the cup and completely surround the tulip. Be careful to fill the area around the petals first to help hold them together. Pouring the silica too quickly could cause the petals to open in an unattractive way.

Flowers will dry very quickly in silica, and knowing just how long to leave the individual flowers in the silica gel is difficult. Each flower you pick retains a different amount of water; it is impossible to know an exact drying time in advance. Most flowers will dry in three to four days, but it is important to check often. You might find it helpful to mark the date on the outside of the container or box. The flowers will feel crisp to the touch when they are ready to be removed. If left in the gel too long, flowers become faded and drop their petals. To uncover the flower, slowly pour some of the gel out of the container. Then gently lift the flower from the gel and dust it off with a soft artist's brush to remove any additional powder.

One disadvantage of silica gel is that the dried flowers are extremely brittle, so the petals break off easily. To help provide support, apply a dab of clear glue to the underside of the flower head where the petals meet. Silica gel–dried flowers are more likely to reabsorb moisture and become limp quickly if exposed to moist air. To avoid this problem, store the dried flowers away from dampness or high humidity.

Warning: Silica gel has a powdery consistency and can irritate your mucus membranes. Wear a surgical mask and use only in well-ventilated areas.

FLOWERS TO DRY IN SILICA GEL

Latin Name	Common Name
Althea	hollyhock
Calluna	heather
Clematis	clematis
Consolida	larkspur
Delphinium	delphinium
Digitalis	foxglove
Echinacea	coneflower
Echinops	globe thistle
Erica	heath
Helianthus	sunflower
Narcissus	daffodils
Paeonea	peony
Papaver	poppy
Rosa	rose
Tagetes	marigold
Trachymene coerulea	blue lace flower
Tulipa	tulip
Viola	pansy
Viola	violet

GLYCERINE

The most effective way to preserve foliage is to use a solution of glycerine and water. This leaves foliage looking naturally moist and supple. Glycerine is also quite effective for preserving plants that become brittle when dry. Seedpods such as Chinese lanterns and flowers such as statice and baby's breath will benefit from this treatment. You can purchase glycerine from a chemical supply company or a local pharmacy. Pick plants that are unblemished and have not begun to show signs of autumn color. Glycerine is not easily absorbed into new growth or by plants that are too mature; for this reason it is best to choose foliage in its midseason or peak. Glycerine tends to turn leaves a darker green and occasionally it turns them a wonderful burgundy color. For example, I placed *leucothoe* into a glycerine solution container and was delighted with the resulting rich bronze color.

To prepare plants for the glycerine solution, crush the stems at the bottom ½ inch, or strip them with a sharp knife. Then soak the stems for 24 hours in a mixture of 1 tablespoon salt and a gallon of warm water. These steps will help the stem absorb the glycerine solution. Mix 1 part glycerine to 2 parts hot water. (Reheat the solution after use to make it more effective.) Stand the stem in a container with 4 inches of the glycerine solution. As the solution is drawn up into the stem, it preserves the leaves. Check daily to see if the solution has all been absorbed and replenish if necessary. When the leaves become soft, leathery and darker in color, they are preserved. They will then last for many months in a dried arrangement.

To preserve an individual leaf, place the entire leaf into a container of the glycerine solution and cover the container. This method is also useful for *Mahonia, Bergenia,* rhododendron and even an entire strand of ivy. Use a weight (such as a stone or small brick) to hold the material down and to ensure that the solution surrounds

Foliage dried in glycerine has a golden beige color.

all parts of the foliage. A drop of green food coloring can be added to preserve the vibrant green of natural foliage. The preserving time varies from one to three weeks. Check daily to see if the leaves are ready.

PLANTS TO PRESERVE IN GLYCERINE

Latin Name	***Common Name***
Adiantum capillus-veneris	maidenhair fern
Buxus sempervierns	common box
Calluna vulgaris	heather
Eucalyptus	eucalyptus
Hedera spp.	ivy
Leucothoe	leucothoe
Magnolia	magnolia
Moluccella laevis	bells of Ireland
Quercus spp.	oak

PRESSING

Once the most popular way to preserve cherished flowers was to press them between the pages of a book or bible. This was also the method used during scientific expeditions as a way to preserve and later study plant material. Because dried leaves do not reabsorb moisture, many wonderful remains from Roman times, such as laurel crowns once worn during ceremonies, have been uncovered and still remain in good condition. Today, pressed flowers are used for decoration. Some dried materials, such as ferns, are nice additions to dried arrangements. Most often, however, we mount and frame pressed flowers.

When looking for flowers to press, remember that the ones with a single row of petals such as pansies, violets and larkspur usually work best. Avoid meaty, thick flowers such as roses, camellias and mums. If the center of a flower is too dense and meaty, you may need to remove the center and press the petals only. You can air-dry the center and reassemble the flower by gluing the petals back on after pressing. To flatten smaller centers, gently press them between your thumb and forefinger. The best way to find out which flowers can be successfully pressed is to experiment.

Press only flowers that are free of damage caused by insects or disease. Also, choose a plant suitable for pressing and select a bud, an open flower and a leaf or piece of foliage. This allows you to preserve the different stages of the plant, from bud to final flower head. Spread the leaves or flowers onto an absorbent piece of paper. Special blotting paper can be used, but paper towels

One of the oldest forms of preserving flowers is with a flower press. Here pansies and violets are placed on blotting paper, waiting to be pressed.

For pressing larger flowers or foliage, place them between several sheets of newspaper and weigh them down with a brick or another heavy object.

will do the job. (Use paper towels that don't have ridges, as these will mark your finished flowers.) Make sure the plant material does not overlap and touch. This will prevent the bleeding of color and uneven pressure. Insert the absorbent paper with the plant material between the pages of a book. The thickness of the paper will determine how many pages should go between each set of flowers. If the paper is thin, use three sheets between each set to avoid bleeding of color. Write the name of the pressed material and the date on each page. This is an important step because it is often difficult to identify the plant once it has dried. Place a brick on top to provide adequate pressure. Most flowers will take four to six weeks to dry, depending on such factors as thickness of the flower petals. Keep a close watch and transfer flowers onto fresh, dry blotting paper if necessary.

Telephone books are good for drying. They're cheap, plentiful, and have absorbent pages. This means you probably won't even need to use paper towels. If you bring the phone book right out into the garden, you can place your flowers directly into it (which lessens the chances of delicate petals being blown apart). When you open the telephone book to check your flowers, remember to start from the back of the book. The pressure will hold the other flowers flat.

For larger plants, use several sheets of newspaper. The foliage of many plants, such as ferns and astilbe, dry beauti-

You can purchase a flower press like this one or build one.

fully using this method. Follow the directions given above for layering each page. Cover with more sheets of newspaper. Allow about 10 pages between each filled page. Continue to layer leaves and paper, and finish by putting a weight on top.

You can also press flowers with a flower press. A press is two same-size pieces of wood held together by screws or straps, which can be opened or held together tightly. When you use a flower press, place an absorbent material (such as paper towels) between the pressed material layers. It takes two to three weeks to preserve flowers when using a press, and some of the natural color is lost in the process.

The best way to achieve the most natural-looking finished flower is to dry it as quickly as possible. You can speed up the pressed flower process by combining it with the silica gel method. The end result will be a more colorful and natural-looking pressed flower. Place the flower in silica gel (see silica gel method, page 25) for approximately half the required time. Then press the flower between the pages of a telephone book, or pressing boards. As with all drying methods, it is important to check after several days for signs of dryness. Close the press and continue the process if the material does not appear adequately dry.

Once your material is completely dry, it is time to mount it onto a backing board. Select a mounting board of linen, velour or velvet, or a matting board of the type used by picture framers. You can use a silicone adhesive to mount the flowers onto the backing board. If the flowers are small and delicate, a pair of tweezers will help to position them on the board. Avoid using household glues because they can cause discoloration after framing.

Working with silicone adhesives can be messy, so some people prefer to place the flowers onto the backing board and cover them with a sheet of clear contact paper. Start by cutting a sheet of contact paper slightly larger than the backboard. Adhere the top of the contact paper to your working surface or table. Slowly smooth the contact paper downward and outward over the flowers on the backboard. Work slowly because the petals will often jump off the backboard due to the static nature of the plastic contact paper.

FLOWERS TO PRESS

Latin Name	**Common Name**
Alchemilla	lady's mantle
Anemone	anemone
Astrantia	masterwort
Clematis	clematis
Consolida	larkspur
Daucus carota	love-in-a-mist
Delphinium	Delphinium
Dicentra	bleeding-heart
Hydrangea	hydrangea
Lonicera	honeysuckle
Primula	primrose
Rosa	rose
Viola	pansy

FOLIAGE AND LEAVES TO PRESS

Latin Name	**Common Name**
Acer palmatum	Japanese maple
Artemisia	wormwood
Clematis	clematis
Ferns	ferns
Fraxinus	ash
Gramineae spp.	grasses
Hedera	ivy
Ilex	holly
Laurus	bay

DRYING IN A MICROWAVE OVEN

The newest way to dry flowers is in the microwave oven. Some flowers can be dried by simply placing them between several layers of microwaveable paper towels and heating for three to five minutes. If your microwave has a setting of 2 to 10, use 4. If it has a range of defrost to high, use the defrost setting. Allow the microwaved flowers to stand for 10 minutes, and then check for dryness. Most flowers, however, will need to be covered by silica gel before being placed in the microwave. The heat of the microwave speeds the absorption of moisture by the silica gel. Almost any flower that can be air-dried can be successfully dried in a microwave oven. It is also the best way to dry extra stems. Real stems give your arrangements a more natural look than stems made from florist's wire wrapped in tape.

Microwave ovens vary slightly and each type of flower dries at a different rate, so you will have to experiment to find the correct amount of time needed. Stay close to your microwave oven and check often. Place similar flowers in the microwave together, and make sure that they do not touch. Most flowers are best dried facing up. Start by putting 1½ inches of silica gel on the bottom of a microwaveable container. Place the flower or foliage on top of the silica gel layer (be sure to allow 1¼ inches between the sides of the container and the plant material). Gently sprinkle silica gel around the plant material until it covers all surfaces evenly. Place the uncovered container into the microwave.

The drying time for several flowers generally is two to two and a half minutes. But the density of the petals and the size of the flower will determine the drying time, so it is important to check often during the process. The flowers will feel brittle or dry to the touch when they are ready.

After being microwaved, the plant material will require a standing time. Like food cooked by microwaves, the flowers will continue to dry even after the microwave oven has been shut off. Allow the flowers to remain in the microwave oven for approximately one minute after it has been shut off. For fragile and delicate flowers, a standing time outside the microwave of about 10 minutes should be adequate. Fuller flowers will often take 30 minutes.

When the standing time is over, carefully empty the container onto a piece of dry newspaper and gently lift the plant material. Remove excess silica gel from sturdy flowers by gently shaking the flowers. For delicate flowers, you will need a oft paintbrush to remove the xcess. Then check the center f the flower to make sure that is completely dry; if not, over this area with silica gel nd reheat it in the microwave ven for a short time. (Allow he silica gel to return to room emperature before reusing.)

FLOWERS TO DRY IN A MICROWAVE OVEN

atin Name	Common Name
chillea millefolium	yarrow
lthaea rosea	hollyhock
nemone coronaria	poppy anemone
nethum graveolens	dill
quilegia hybrid	columbine
Astilbe hybrid	astilbe
Astrantia major	masterwort
Centaurea montana	mountain bluet
Chrysanthemum parthenium	feverfew
Dahlia spp.	dahlia
Delphinium ajacis	annual larkspur
Delphinium hybrid	delphinium
Digitalis purpurea	foxglove
Erica gracilis	heath
Eupatorium purpureum	Joe Pye weed
Heuchera sanguinea	coralbells
Hydrangea macrophylla	French hydrangea
H. paniculata	hydrangea
Narcissus	daffodil
Rosa	rose
Rudbeckia purpurea	purple coneflower
Sedum spectabile	sedum
Solidago canadensis	goldenrod
Syringa	lilac
Tagetes	marigold
Tulipa	tulip
Viola	pansy
Zinnia	zinnia

Caution: If a flower has a delicate stem that needs to be supported by wire, you must do this after the flower has been removed from the microwave oven. Do not put metal in a microwave oven.

STORING DRIED FLOWERS

o further preserve dried flowrs (regardless of the drying nethod), spray them lightly vith a dried flower preservaive. There are several commerial sprays made expressly for his purpose. However, I find airspray to be just as effecive. Dried berries and seedods can be dipped into a jar f shellac. Store your dried lowers, berries and seedpods n a dry, dark area. This helps hem maintain their natural

t is easier and faster to create our dried arrangements if you tore dried flowers of like colors ogether.

Store delicate dried flowers on wire racks.

A drying/storage room should be free of moisture and excessive daylight.

color. Some light is acceptable as long as it does not shine directly on the dried flowers. To protect your dried flowers from excessive sunlight, store them in closed containers between layers of tissue paper. Label and date the individual boxes. Try to use the oldest materials first to ensure freshness.

Even in the best of situations, problems can arise during storage. A tiny weevil-like insect (possibly brought in on one of the plants) may lay its eggs in the warmth of the drying room. The eggs will hatch and the insects will eat the dry petals. Checking your plants carefully for insects before drying can help. However, many insects are so tiny that they are impossible to detect until the damage has already occurred. Place the infested flowers in airtight containers and place into a freezer for 24 hours; the cold temperature kills the insects. To prevent insects from damaging your dried flowers, add mothballs to the containers and place insect traps around the drying room. These traps can be purchased at your hardware store or garden center.

Coat Hangers

Coat hangers make great holders for air-drying flowers or for storing already dried flowers. Wind an elastic band around a small bunch of flowers. Put the stems behind the hanger and pull the second loop forward, up and over the stems. The bunches will remain attached to the coat hanger and the rubber bands will tighten as the stems shrink. To remove the bunches, just pull downward. An attic or a warm closet with rods or heating pipes are ideal places to hang these bunches.

PURCHASING DRIED PLANTS

If space is limited or you simply don't have the time to prowl the roadsides and meadows for drying materials, you can buy them. In some cases, it is actually more cost effective to purchase dried materials. Statice, for example, is inexpensive and is available in a wide range of colors; although easy to grow, it tends to take up too much space in the garden. Flowers that are difficult to grow, such as roses and lavender, can also be bought fresh. Most store-bought flowers can be dried using one of the six basic methods.

To preserve berries or rose hips, dip them into clear shellac and hang them up to dry.

4

DESIGNING WITH DRIED FLOWERS

INTRODUCTION TO DRIED FLOWER ARRANGING

If you learned all the rules of flower arranging and applied them all to every arrangement, it would be nothing short of a miracle. It would also take the fun out of flower arranging. So be sure to follow this one simple rule: Arrange flowers in such a way that they will please you.

There are countless books on flowers, and every magazine has photos of arrangements. Take notice of the ones you like best. Start by creating simple arrangements, then move on to more complicated arrangements as your skills and confidence increase. For example, you might want to use a single color with varying shades and foliage in your first arrangement. Arrangements can be as simple as a small bunch of *Celosia* placed in an old teapot or as intricate as a large mass arrangement composed of a number of different flowers, berries and dried pods. The most important thing to remember is that there are no set rules in dried flower arranging; any combination of flowers that pleases you is a perfect arrangement!

Working with dried flowers can be challenging because they are very brittle and apt to break easily. Their colors also tend to be more subtle than those of fresh flowers, and will fade even further with age and exposure to light. However, dried flower arranging has advantages over fresh flower arranging, too. One advantage is that you can take several days to create a dried arrangement. You will also have a good selection of plant material from which to choose. Mix and match beauties of all seasons, such as a spring-flowering branch of dogwood with the gorgeous roses of summer and even the dried hydrangea of autumn. It is always fun to create such mixed-season arrangements because they truly are tributes to the beauty and variety of your garden.

Before you begin to place flowers, think out and plan the arrangement. If you change your mind too often, you'll end up with an unstable floral foam base that is full of holes, as well as flowers that are so beat up you cannot use them properly. In your planning, remember that the ultimate goal is to achieve harmony of color, proportion and feeling among the flowers, container and setting.

Dried flower arrangements can be made in many different types of containers. In fact, collecting unusual containers can become a hobby in itself! Be on the lookout at flea markets, garage sales and Grandma's attic. Containers with chips and cracks, and even those missing parts (such as a teacup without a handle, or a teapot without the top) can be quite lovely. The container almost always dictates the size, shape and style of your final arrangement. The basic rule of thumb is that arrangements should be one and a half to two times the height of the container. It is also important to choose a container that is in proportion to the spot where it will rest. For example, you would not want a wide, full ar-

Dried flowers can be used in a variety of ways throughout the year. Here a small holiday tree is adorned with tiny dried rose buds and dried berries.

Be on the lookout for interesting containers for your dried arrangements. An old tea cup looks lovely filled with dried rose buds.

One-sided bouquets work well on small tables or narrow mantels.

rangement on a narrow hall table. Instead, one that is narrow and possibly flat on the back side would fit nicely in such a setting. Tall, narrow containers can be used to create dramatic vertical arrangements that don't require a great deal of space. They can add a special touch to a narrow table or countertop.

Use your judgment to determine a pleasing balance between containers and flowers. Choose flowers that complement the container in size and shape, as well as color. When making a natural or informal arrangement, it is best to use a basket, copper or other metal container, or a solid-color container, which will blend in and not overpower the tans and browns of the dried material. If you select a large, open bowl, you will need a lot of flowers and filler materials to cover the open area and hide the foam base. If you don't have many flowers, try a container with a small opening, such as an old, colored glass bottle. Large, heavy-headed flowers will overpower small, delicate containers.

SOME OF MY FAVORITE CONTAINERS

Baskets
Bowls
Clay flowerpots
Jars
Mugs
Old hatboxes
Old hats
Paper bags
Soup tureens
Teapots (old or broken)
Tin cans (old paint cans)
Umbrella stands
Wooden boxes or crates

Color is an essential element of dried arrangements. Often the colors will be determined by the color scheme of the room in which the arrangement will be placed. The eye gives different emphasis to different colors and different sizes. Bright colors, for example, will stand out more than pale colors, and large flowers will stand out more than small ones. Dark flowers seem heavier than lighter-colored flowers of equal size and height. Because of this, you might find it best to place lighter-colored flowers higher up in the arrangement, while placing the darker, larger flowers toward the base. No one questions Mother Nature's judgment when she mixes many vibrant colors in a summer wildflower meadow. So if you love to mix strong colors in arrangements, I see no reason why you shouldn't. But the color mix in each arrangement will be different, so be sure to look at the relationship of the colors to each other.

You can achieve harmony in your design by using plant material to help blend colors together. Green, which is ever-present in nature, is extremely useful in dried arrangements. The many variations, from the pale yellow-green to the deep blue-green, all help unify your finished arrangement. The veins and subtle hints of other color in your dried material will also help to blend the arrangement.

To give your arrangement a natural appearance, use flowers of different heights. Cut or lengthen stems of similar flowers so that they are varying

An arrangement of dried flowers in an antique porcelain bowl.

Once you decide on your container, begin placing a few strategic flowers. Your final arrangement will develop from this starting point.

The final arrangement can contain many different textures and colors, but it should always appear pleasing to the eye.

This arrangement has a pleasing shape and the colors complement each other beautifully.

heights. Before you cut the stems, hold them close to the spot where you plan to place them. Let your eye judge the best height and angle. This prevents unnatural and stiff-looking lines in the arrangement. Also, use odd numbers of flowers. Odd numbers seem to create a more pleasing effect. You can easily test this theory. First, place just two flowers in a vase. Next place three flowers in a vase. Which looks better to you?

Once you have decided on your color scheme, container and general theme, you can begin. To keep everything tidy, do your arranging on a flat piece of plastic such as a garbage bag. First fit your Oasis or floral foam tightly into the container and secure with floral tape to prevent it from shifting around. The first flowers to place are the taller ones, which will define the height and shape of the arrangement. Also, try to add flowers with thick stems early on to avoid damaging more delicate flowers. Place very delicate flowers last to avoid rough handling. When you have finished placing the flowers, add filler material such as *Gypsophila* to fill in any holes and give a finished look. When you are working on the arrangement, step back occasionally and look at it from all angles. If it's to be a centerpiece, walk around it and view it from the back and sides. If it's to sit on a mantel, look at it from below.

Keep your arrangement three-dimensional. The best flowers should be in the front line and the secondary flowers behind them. Flowers with slight imperfections can be added to the display at a low, protected level. For the sake of balance, you might want to use heavier flowers at the base of the arrangement. Don't allow these heavier stems to extend out horizontally from the arrangement; keep them anchored for a stable appearance. Set some of the lighter and smaller flowers toward the ends of the arrangement. Vary the angle at which you place stems so they will not all be on one plane.

It is important to leave space between flowers because you do not want them to appear crowded. Be sure your eye can move in and out of an arrangement. The most interesting display will have one flower peeking out from behind another, with a third almost hidden in the depths, and a fourth springing out from behind them even to the edge of the arrangement. For arrangements that will be displayed on mantels or other high points, use some flowers with stems that droop. Secure the foam base so that it peeks out about ¼ inch over the top of the container. Then place short-stemmed flowers to loll over the rim. The same technique is useful for centerpieces.

As you near the end, carefully appraise the arrangement. Do you need another flower here or there, or do you have enough? Should you take a flower away? If a flower seems out of place, take it out. But be careful not to disturb the arrangement. The easiest way to remove it may be to snip off the stem where it won't show, instead of pulling out the whole flower.

BASIC STEPS FOR ARRANGING

. After choosing the con-
ainer, add a support (or base)
o fit securely inside. A block
f floral foam or a circle of
hicken wire fitted tightly into
he bottom of the container will
vork as a support. Secure the
upport to the side of the con-
ainer with floral tape. This
mportant step prevents the ar-
angement from becoming top
eavy. If neither floral foam
or chicken wire is available,
ıse fine sand (a centuries-old
nethod) as a support. Simply
ill the container three-quarters
ull with dry fine sand.
. Create the outline of the ar-
angement using taller spiky
lowers. The stems of the flow-
rs should not be all the same length because this would give an unnatural appearance.
3. Add tiny bunches of interesting material such as *Nigella* pods and secure them with wire onto a florist's pick before adding.
4. For a final touch you may add some special flowers or pods. Place uneven numbers of these throughout the arrangement.
5. Place your filler material, such as German statice or baby's breath, to fill in holes and give a finished look.
6. Because of the brittle nature of dried flowers, spray the finished arrangement with a preservative.

Fragrance in Dried Arrangements

Fragrance can make an arrangement unique. Don't overlook your herb collection for possible fragrant candidates. Artemisia, dill, the blooms of basil, catmint, lavender, Calimentha *and hyssop are all easily air-dried for arranging.*

Foliage and flowers that hold their scent when dried:

Anethum graveolens	dill
Artemisia annua	sweet Annie
Foeniculum vulgare	fennel
Lavandula	lavender
Thymus	thyme

STYLES OF DRIED FLOWER ARRANGEMENTS

Simple Mass Arrangement

Creating an arrangement of dried flowers can be as simple as choosing a container and filling it to the brim with one variety of dried flower. Such simple arrangements are often quite dramatic. Fill a basket with flowers such as baby's breath, sea lavender or German statice to create a full arrangement. For added interest, insert vials of seasonal fresh flowers or other more colorful dried flowers. These arrangements will last for many months if you just freshen up the accent flowers every few weeks.

Traditional Arrangement

Traditional dried arrangements resemble fresh flower arrangements. The first step is to place the foliage material as a background; this will also create the overall shape. Next add filler materials, which will provide texture to the arrangement. Finally, incorporate the more prominent and colorful flowers such as dahlias, peonies or roses.

This pitcher is filled with dried hydrangea. Using a single flower provides a most dramatic arrangement.

This one-sided bouquet was collected while fresh and hung to dry.

Baskets are beautiful and useful. A small basket is decorated with dried flowers around the rim and filled with fragrant potpourri.

One-sided Bouquet

A traditional, one-sided, fan-shaped bouquet of dried flowers is easy to make and is useful on a narrow table and a mantel. This versatile style is comfortable on a table with its back to the wall, decorating the top of a wrapped gift or hanging upside down on a wall. It is sometimes best to create this fan-shaped arrangement with fresh flowers before hanging them to dry. By using fresh flowers you can work without causing damage to the brittle dried flowers. To make a flat-sided bouquet, start with the tallest flowers or foliage (such as artemisia) as the bottom layer. This layer needs to be full enough to support the flowers that will be placed on top. Lay the first layer on a table in a fan shape. Cross over the stems at the bottom. Next, add a layer of flowers that are slightly shorter so the bottom layer shows around the edges and on top. Gradually layer on top more foliage and flowers. Make sure that each layer is visible. Tightly wind a rubber band around all the stems at the end. This step is important because flowers shrink during the drying process. Add final touches after drying, if necessary. The finished bouquet is tied with a ribbon (or raffia, for an informal bouquet) to hide the rubber band.

Nosegays

Nosegays or tussie mussies are fun to create and make wonderful gifts. They can be made with fresh or dried flowers. A certain amount of stress will cause the dry stems to break. Caution should be taken when working with all dried material for this reason. For fresh flowers, see the list on page 00 of flowers that air-dry well. Collect the flowers one by one and hold them tightly in your hand while intertwining their stems in a crisscross pattern. When you are pleased with the combinations of color and textures, wrap the stems together with a rubber band or a piece of wire high up and close to the flower heads. If fresh flowers were used, hang the bouquet upside down until dry. After it is dry it will be strong enough to stand up on a dresser or table without the support of a container. Before placing it on a table, tie a pretty ribbon or raffia around the rubber band. Tiny nosegays can also be used to decorate a narrow mantle or as favors on a dinner table.

Decorating Baskets with Dried Flowers

If you would like to decorate a basket, attach a nosegay of dried flowers to the front or handle. For a more dramatic look, twist the fresh flowers of loves-lies-bleeding around the handle of a large basket, where it will air-dry naturally. The foliage and seedpods of autumn can also add seasonal interest. Another way to adorn your basket is to glue or wire dried flowers and foliage onto the basket rim. The basket will be both attractive and useful when filled with guest towels, soaps, potpourri or other goodies.

Pictured are just a few of the many items that can be adorned with dried flowers.

This dried wreath has a rustic natural look. Note the use of birch bark and the artificial bird to create interest.

Wreaths

Wreaths can easily be decorated with dried flowers, berries and other dried material. Once associated only with Christmas, wreaths are now used year 'round, both indoors and out. Try placing small wreaths on tabletops or around the bases of hurricane lamps or candlesticks.

I suggest purchasing ready-made wreath frames. They come in many sizes and shapes and are made of materials such

Remember to save all fallen and broken dried petals to use in potpourri mixes. Potpourri is easy and fun to make. It is a wonderful gift.

Potpourri

Always save petals that break off flowers during the drying and arranging process. Keep all of the dried debris after cleaning out your drying room at the end of the season. These "scraps" can all be added to your potpourri. Some of the flowers (lavender, mint, scented geranium and eucalyptus leaves, for example) have long-lasting fragrance. Essential oils will heighten or add fragrance to the mixture. Show off your potpourri in an attractive container, small bowl, tiny basket or even an antique tea cup.

POTPOURRI

2 cups dried rose petals
½ cup dried lemon mint leaves
¼ cup dried scented geranium leaves
3 tablespoons crushed dried lemon and orange peel
5 drops rose-scented essential oil

Mix together all ingredients. Seal in a dry plastic bag. Place the bag in a cool, dark place for six weeks. Shake the bag several times once it is sealed and occasionally during the six-week period to mix the oils and petals. Remove the potpourri from the bag and put it into an attractive container. Whole flowers or petals can be placed on top for display. The fun of potpourri is that you can create many different fragrances by adding or changing the ingredients. Pinecones and evergreen needles, for example, add a fresh winter scent. To refresh the fragrance, sprinkle a few drops of essential oils on a small cotton ball, and tuck it into the potpourri mixture.

Swags of dried flowers can be used to decorate mantels or staircases.

This swag of dried hydrangea, gomphrena, and baby's breath is wrapped with gold silk braiding and used to decorate a mantel for Christmas.

as straw, grapevines, floral foam and wire. The first step in making a dried flower wreath is to cover the entire frame with a base material such as moss, artemisia, statice or lavender. These base materials can be added while they are still fresh and pliable, and they can dry on the frame. My favorite dried wreath is one covered with sea lavender. This lavender, which I collect in late summer, grows along the shoreline. I wire together tiny bunches and secure each bunch to the frame with wire or clear fishing line. A sea lavender wreath is lovely by itself, or with the added color of a ribbon. If you want to add more colorful flowers or other materials over your base material, allow several days for the base material to dry. Once it has dried attach additional flowers with wire or floral picks. Work in the same direction, and go around the entire wreath. Complete the wreath with a pretty ribbon or bow.

Swags and Garlands

Swags and garlands are wonderful additions to any decor. Drape them over a dresser or down the length of a dining table, or hang them over a mantel, mirror, doorway, entrance or headboard. Start by measuring the area where the swag will hang. Remember to keep swags of dried material well away from fire or extreme heat where they may be a fire hazard. Use a sturdy base constructed of wire, heavy woven jute or a Styrofoam form. Wire together two lush branches cut to size for a natural-looking swag base. Attached at the middle, they naturally provide small twig shapes that will serve as bases for the dried flowers to be wired or glued onto. The winter holidays are a perfect time to use evergreen roping for your base. It is sold at garden centers by the yard.

Wire several dried flowers together to form bouquets. It is best to make all of the small bouquets out of the same flowers. Lay the individual bouquets along the swag base and secure each with a piece of wire long enough to be twisted along the entire length of the swag. If you like, ribbons or bows can be incorporated into swags as you go. Swags can be made to celebrate each season: spring, summer, autumn and winter.

Topiary

Small topiaries or standards can be used as table decorations. If you have a live topiary such as an ivy, rosemary or santolina growing in a pot, just add individual dried flowers or small bouquets to give it a decorative look for parties or holidays. In winter, add dried berries, small seed heads, pods, or pinecones to create a seasonal topiary.

You can buy mock topiary forms from floral supply stores or create your own. To make a topiary form, you will need a base container such as a clay pot, vase or basket fitted with a piece of floral foam. Remember to tape the foam securely to the container. You will also need a stem, which can be a stick, branch or short wooden dowel. Secure the stem into the base container with floral tape. Finally, you will need to attach your chosen topiary shape onto the stem. Cover the floral foam ball with a base or filler flower such as moss or sea lavender. The base material can be attached with floral pins or glue. Once the form is covered completely, add interesting and colorful dried flowers such as rosebuds, bachelor buttons, zinnias or pods and berries. For a final touch, have thin strands of silk or velvet ribbon stream down, or tie on tiny ribbon bows. Hold the ribbons in place with floral pins or hairpins.

Floral Ball or Kissing Ball

Traditional kissing balls were covered with mistletoe. They hung in doorways or from chandeliers during the Christmas holidays. Floral supply stores sell round floral forms to use as a base for these quaint balls. Cover the form with a base material such as sweet Annie (or, of course, mistletoe). Then add colorful flowers and possibly ribbon. If you'd like to hang the dried flower ball from a doorway or chandelier, tie a length of ribbon or string around the ball or secure it to the ball with a long, straight pin. The floral ball can also be used sitting in a pretty bowl or dish. Remember to keep the flowers in scale with the size of the floral foam ball and the container that it will finally sit in.

Christmas Tree

You can buy a tree-shaped form made of Styrofoam, wire or grapevines at most floral supply stores. Dried material can be tucked into the forms or glued on top of them. Use a base material (such as moss, artemisia or baby's breath) first and then add the more colorful flowers as accents. Another method is to purchase a live small tree to use on a tabletop or mantel. Wire together tiny bunches of dried flowers and attach them to the tree. Individual rosebuds, sprigs of baby's

This decorative Christmas tree is made of dried hydrangea, gomphrena, and celosia. A few strands of satin ribbon complete the festive look.

breath and colorful dried berries are also nice accents. For a final touch, you might add tiny colored bows or tiny wrapped packages.

Framed Pressed Flowers

For centuries, pressed flowers have been displayed in picture frames. A collection of antique silver or wooden frames make wonderful accents for displaying pressed flowers. Pictures made from pressed flowers can be as simple as a single petal or blossom or as elaborate as a large bouquet or intricate landscape. The more intricate pictures are created by adding many tiny petals and individual flowers. This is a very delicate project and you will need to make a sketch before you begin your design. Start by putting a tiny bit of glue on a toothpick and lightly dabbing it on the back of the flower or petal. Using tweezers, gently position the flowers onto the backing board. Allow your picture to dry overnight. Check for edges that need to be secured before placing glass on top. Seal the edges of the backing board and glass with clear tape to keep out excessive moisture. Finally, fit the mounted flowers into frames. Pressed flowers can also be used to decorate invitations and ordinary note cards.

Hats Decorated with Dried Flowers

Fold back the brim of a large-brimmed hat and attach a bouquet of dried flowers with a hat pin. If your hat doesn't have a wide brim, glue dried flowers onto the hat band. Keep a tiny bouquet of dried flowers wired to a hat pin on your dresser, so you can quickly change the mood of any hat you choose. Dried autumn leaves and berries make wonderful decorations for winter hats.

Dried berries make a pleasing addition to this black felt hat.

Small silver picture frames are used to display individual pressed flowers. Johnny jump-ups, coreopsis, larkspur, and dianthus are shown here.

SUPPLIES FOR DRYING AND ARRANGING

For arranging and creating projects, I have set up a large wooden table in the garage. This spot is close to the drying room and away from the daily activities of the family. A kitchen table can be used but it is better to have a spot that can be left with all your supplies and materials. You will almost certainly need some of the following supplies:

Dried Flower Oasis (Floral Foam): Sierra Oasis is brown and harder than green Oasis (which is soaked in water and used to arrange fresh flowers). It is available in blocks, balls, and sometimes wreath shapes. It can be cut using a blunt knife to any shape desired.

Chicken Wire: Chicken wire provides extra support for taller, top-heavy flowers. It can be fitted into a container and used as a stem support. Chicken wire can also be stretched over the top of a container to keep individual stems separated during the upright air-drying method.

Floral Wire: Floral wire comes in many different gauges and you will need several gauges for most projects. It can be used to reinforce flower stems, to attach tiny clusters of flowers to floral picks, and to extend stems. To add strength to flower heads, I use green florist wire, 20-inch gauge. It is best to wire flowers before they are dried, except for microwave-dried flowers. If the stems will be seen, attach a sturdy stem from a different flower. You can dry most any sturdy stem in the microwave (see page 30).

Clear Fishing Line: This is the one supply I consider absolutely essential. Because it is invisible and very strong, it has many uses. Not only is it useful for creating dry flower arrangements, but it is invaluable for many projects throughout the garden.

Floral Tape: Floral tape is dark green and elastic with a gum base. It is easy to work with because it can be stretched to cover reinforcing wire or to attach a hollow stem. Floral tape is also useful for securing Sierra foam to containers.

Floral Picks: These pointed wooden sticks with wire attached to them resemble large toothpicks. They are used to secure flowers to base frames.

Glue Stick or Hot Glue Gun: Both of these are used to attach individual flowers to a base or affix dried flowers to any surface. Use caution with glue guns because the glue becomes very hot and can burn your skin.

Wire Cutter: Use cutters to trim florist wire to desired length.

Manicure Scissors: These tiny scissors are helpful when you need to trim out some discoloration or problem on a dried flower.

Needle-Nose Pliers: Use these pliers to help insert flowers into an arrangement that has been wired or secured to a pick.

Tweezers: Tweezers allow you to gently pick up and position pressed flowers onto a backing board.

Varnish: Clear varnish is used to preserve berries and rose hips. Quickly dip the hips or berries into the can of varnish and hang to drip-dry.

Protective Spray: There are many preservative sprays available that prevent moisture absorption. I use hairspray as my preservative and find it works very well.

Moss: There are two kinds of moss readily available. Decorator moss is sold in bags and it unrolls in sheets. It can be cut to any desired size for covering bare soil, or gluing onto baskets or plastic containers. It has been harvested and air-dried to preserve its natural green color and beauty. Spanish moss is harvested in long grayish silver strands. It grows naturally in the South, where it hangs from trees in great masses. It can be used to hide the soil in containers or at the base of flower arrangements and it can be used as fillers on wreaths.

5

PLANT PORTRAITS

THE MANY FACES OF DRIED FLOWERS

You may be surprised by the vast number of flowers, herbs, shrubs, roses and vines that can be easily dried. In this chapter I have listed a variety of plants for drying based on the flowers they produce, as well as their attractive berries, seed heads and foliage. Most of the plants are easy to grow and reliable to air-dry. However, for the adventurous, I have included some flowers that are a bit more of a challenge to both grow and preserve.

PLANT PORTRAIT KEY

Here is a guide to the symbols and terms used throughout this section.

Latin name of the plant is in boldface italic type.

Phonetic pronunciation of the Latin name is in parentheses.

Common name of the plant is in boldface type.

The average hours of sun needed per day is indicated by symbols. The first symbol is what the plant prefers, but the plant is adaptable to all conditions listed.

○ *Sun*—Six hours or more of direct sunlight per day.
◐ *Part shade*—Three to six hours of direct sunlight per day.
● *Shade*—Two hours or less of direct sunlight.

Grade of Difficulty: Plants that take the least amount of care are identified as "easy." These plants are good choices for beginning gardeners.

Heights are for normal growth, but plants with very fertile soil may grow taller and those with poor growing conditions may be shorter.

Zones "The USDA Plant Hardiness Map" (page 00) is based on average annual temperatures for each area (zone) of the United States. Check this map to see which zone you live in. Each plant portrait will list the zones best for your chosen shrub, tree or perennial. Annuals do not require zones as they complete their life cycle in one growing season and most can be grown in almost any climate during warmer months.

Cultural Information explains plants' preferences for soil and proper care for growing them.

Harvesting/Drying This section will provide information on the best time to harvest your flowers for drying. It will also provide any special tips needed to have success with each individual flower.

Many common annuals, such as zinnias, dry beautifully and are grown in a wide range of colors.

Most yarrows air-dry easily and are useful fillers for dried arrangements.

The delicate dried flower of Achillea *'The Pearl' provides a soft addition to most arrangements.*

Achillea (a-KIL-lee-a) **yarrow,** easy, perennial. ○
Zones: 3 to 8
Height: 1½ to 4 feet
Colors: White, yellow, shades of pink
Characteristics: Yarrow is a long-blooming and rugged perennial. It will quickly establish handsome colonies in the border. The flowers bloom from June through September. To maintain maximum color, cut flowers that are no more than two days old, because they tend to fade with time. I find that the easiest yarrow to dry is *Achillea filipendulina,* commonly called fern-leaf yarrow. It has striking yellow flower heads that appear on sturdy 4-foot-tall stems. The foliage of yarrow has a lovely fragrance and can be dried and added to potpourri. The pungent foliage can also help deter moths when used in storing winter garments.

A. ptarmica 'The Pearl' is a dwarf variety with lovely double white flowers on 2-foot stems. It has tiny clusters of flowers that can be separated and used in miniature dried arrangements.
Cultural Information: Plant yarrow plants 2½ to 3 feet apart in well-drained soil in fall or late spring after all danger of frost is past. Cut the plant back to a few inches from the ground after harvesting flowers for drying, to help induce bushiness and increase next year's blooms. Divide every three to four years in early spring or late fall. Although these plants are considered drought-resistant, they do appreciate a good watering during dry, hot weather. To avoid stem rot, water the plants early in the day, especially in moist climates. When the plants are several inches high, mulch the soil between them with compost. Compost will decompose in one season. It adds nutrients to the soil, keeps weeds down and conserves moisture. Yarrow is generally pest-free due to the pungent foliage and is easily grown from seed. It is credited with attracting beneficial insects, including ladybugs. Germination takes from 10 to 14 days; the optimal temperature is 65° to 70° F.
Harvesting/Drying: Harvest in late summer when the flowers are fully opened and the heads feel firm to the touch. Hang individual stems in a warm, dark, well-ventilated spot or dry them upright. If space is limited you may tie a small bunch together with a rubber band, but the flower shape is better if each flower is hung individually. Be careful not to crush the flower heads. Dried yarrow is a good filler plant. It makes a

soft, natural, yellow base, which blends well with other dried materials. For a winning combination, combine yarrow with blue salvia. Use in potpourri or as filling for dresser drawer moth bags where its fragrant foliage will help deter moths.
Methods: Air-dry, silica, press, microwave

Acroclinium; see ***Helipterum***

African daisy; see ***Lonas***

Ageratum houstonianum *and* Moluccella *are striking when planted together in the garden.*

Ageratum houstonianum (aj-er-AY-tum hew-ston-ee-AH-num) **floss flower,** easy, annual. ○
Height: 5 to 9 inches for dwarf varieties, 24 to 30 inches for tall varieties
Colors: Dark blue, pale blue, lavender, white, pink
Characteristics: Originally from Mexico and Central America, ageratums thrive in hot summer weather as long as they are well watered. The range of blues, from soft, clear blues and powder blues to rich, dark blues, make ageratums very popular annuals.

There are dwarf, compact and tall, upright varieties. The compact varieties form mounds of fuzzy, tufted blossoms that bloom from early summer to fall. Two excellent dwarf varieties are 'Blue Danube' and 'Pink Powder-Puff', which both make very showy edging plants. However, 'Blue Horizon', a taller variety, is better for use in drying.
Cultural Information: Ageratums thrive in well-drained soil enriched with organic matter. They can be propagated from cuttings, but most are grown from seed. The seed requires light to germinate, so simply press the seed lightly into a moist planting formula. The young plants are very tender and initial growth is slow. After transplanting into the garden, pinch back to encourage fullness. On parts of the West Coast where winters are mild, seed can be planted in late summer for fall bloom. Space dwarf varieties 6 inches apart, tall varieties 12 inches.
Harvesting/Drying: Cut the flowers when fully opened, but before they have begun to brown on the edges. Ageratum air-dry easily: Simply cut the flowers, remove the foliage and hang to dry.
Methods: Air-dry, silica

Alcea rosea (al-KEE-a RO-see-a) **hollyhock,** moderate, biannual. ○
Height: 6 feet
Colors: White, yellow, salmon, red, pink, rose, purple

Alcea rosea, *'Pinafore Mix'*

Alchemilla

Characteristics: Hollyhocks are an old-fashioned favorite. They are available in a wide range of colors and forms—single, double, ruffled and fluted. My favorite is still the original single form, but for drying purposes, the double forms are best. The large flowers, up to 4 inches across, are thickly massed on long stems. Allow them to self-sow about your garden to ensure a continuous supply. Because hollyhocks are tall, they are perfect at the back of the garden, or against a fence or building.
Cultural Information: Hollyhocks do well in most soils, but they prefer a well-drained soil with a pH 6.0 to 8.0. To propagate, sow the seed of hollyhock in midsummer in a partially shaded spot. In autumn or in early spring the seedlings can be transplanted to their garden home.
Harvesting/Drying: Pick the flowers at their peak when the color is still strong and the flowers are fresh. Both double and regular varieties can be air-dried, but they will lose some of their natural color and the flowers will tighten up slightly. Air-dried hollyhocks resemble colorful crepe-paper flowers. If you would like to achieve a more perfect flower shape and color, dry in silica gel. Store in an airtight container after drying.
Methods: Air-dry, silica, microwave

Alchemilla vulgaris (al-kem-ILL-uh) **lady's mantle,** easy, perennial. ○ ◐
Zones: 3 to 8
Height: 6 to 12 inches
Color: Yellow-green
Characteristics: Alchemilla vulgaris is a low-growing, graceful perennial with large, pleated, silvery green leaves. Once grown as a medicinal herb, it is now grown as an ornamental plant. Tiny hairs on the leaves collect rain and dew, which form little silvery beads. In late spring, lady's mantle is covered with small clusters of fragrant, yellow-green flowers. This lovely groundcover grows from 6 to 12 inches tall. Lady's mantle looks pretty planted as a border edging—allow it to spill over onto paths and walkways.
Cultural Information: Lady's mantle thrives in cool weather, part shade and well-drained soil. Sow seeds in a cold frame in early spring. After danger of frost, place the plants 4 to 6 inches apart in the garden. If the flower heads are allowed to go to seed, they will self-sow, creating a crop of tiny plants in early spring. These seedlings can be left or relocated to a new location.
Harvesting/Drying: Cut the flowers for winter bouquets at the peak of bloom for best color, and hang them upside down in a drying room. Because the flowers are so small, they tend to dry quickly. Keep them in a warm spot to speed the drying and to maintain the true green color.

Lady's mantle makes a lovely filler for dried arrangements or base for wreaths and swags. The dried flowers and foliage of lady's mantle look wonderful when combined with tiny pink rosebuds.
Methods: Air-dry, silica, microwave

Allium (AL-lium) **allium,** moderate, bulb. ○
Zones: 4–8
Height: Dwarf–6 inches; giant–5 feet

Allium christophii

Colors: Blue, yellow, white, pink, purple, mauve
Characteristics: The allium is a member of the onion family. Edible alliums such as chives, leek and onion produce interesting flower heads if left to mature on the plant. However, they tend to have a strong onion smell that remains after drying. If you are growing allium for drying purposes, I suggest you plant the ornamental alliums. The dried seed heads resemble the explosion of a fireworks display. They come in all heights, from small to giant, with flower heads ranging from 2 to 10 inches across. Ornamental alliums are available in colors of white, pink, yellow, purple, blue and mauve. Each plant sends up a bare stem, thin and straight, carrying a full, rounded head of flowers. The flower heads are attractive and can be left to dry on the plant for garden interest or brought in for use in winter flower arrangements. To ensure a more perfect seed head, harvest at the height of bloom and hang upside down in a dry, dark closet.

Allium albophilosum produces a 10-inch globe of star-shaped lavender-blue flowers on an 18-inch stem. The seed heads should be picked after petals fall. They are easy to air-dry; just hang in a dark, dry spot. For an even more dramatic effect, dry 'Giganteum', a 4-foot-tall allium that has baseball-sized flowers. Many of the larger flowering ornamental alliums, such as 'Giganteum', are short lived. For a continued supply of 'Giganteum', plant a new crop yearly. 'Christophii' flowers in late summer and has a dramatic seed head that is approximately 7 inches across.
Cultural Information: Alliums thrive in rich, well-worked soil, but they are not fussy and will adjust to most soil types. They are fussy about their drainage, however, and will return if given quick-draining soil.
Harvesting/Drying: The flowers of allium can be cut early in the bud stage, or later when seed heads have developed. Air-dry in small bunches, being careful not to alter their lovely round shape. If space is not a consideration, it is usually best to hang them individually to avoid crushing the flower heads. Alliums take time to dry due to their fleshy stems. Handle them carefully after drying because the flower heads tend to be rather delicate.
Method: Air-dry

Amaranth; see ***Amaranthus***

Amaranthus (am-a-RAN-thus)
amaranth, summer poinsettia, easy, annual. ○
Height: 12 to 15 inches dwarf, 3 to 5 feet taller varieties
Colors: Red, orange, yellow, with multicolored foliage
Characteristics: Amaranths provide wonderful displays of color in the late summer garden. These reliable, showy annuals were grown for medicinal purposes by early American settlers. Many different varieties provide a large range of shapes and colors, from deep red to brilliant yellows. Their bold color makes them hard to use, so they are best used as accent plants. Quick to grow, they can fill and enhance any garden spot. *Amaranthus caudatus,* the tassel-type (love-lies-bleeding), has brilliant red tassels that retain their color for eight weeks. The tassels, which are usually a foot or more in length, droop dramatically over the foliage. You can cut and air-dry the tassels for use in winter arrangements.
Cultural Information: Amaranths are not fussy about the soil in which they grow. As with many of the old reliable annuals, they seem to have better leaf color in poorer soil. Direct sow after all danger of frost is past and the soil is warm. In cooler climates, amaranths can be started indoors. Barely cover the seed, keep the soil moist, and germination should take two to three weeks. When transplanting, be careful not to

Amaranthus caudatus

disturb the roots, because this slows growth. It is best to transplant after night temperatures stay above 50°F. The smaller varieties can be spaced 18 inches apart, while taller varieties need 2 to 3 feet. Amaranths thrive in full sun. They are drought-tolerant and enjoy hot, dry places. Taller varieties appreciate shelter from wind.
Harvesting/Drying: Harvest when the plant is in full flower stage. Amaranths can be hung in small bunches to dry. The striking flowers dry nicely and retain much of their original color.

A. caudatus is best dried in an upright position so that it will retain its drooping habit when used in arrangements. It looks wonderful woven into swags or encircling wreaths.
Methods: Air-dry, water-dry

Ammobium (am-O-bee-um)

everlasting, sand flower, winged everlasting, tender perennial. ○
Height: 1 to 2 feet
Color: White
Characteristics: Winged everlastings are wonderful additions to the summer garden. Their tiny white daisylike flowers bloom profusely from July to October if deadheaded. The flowers are about 1 inch across with glistening white petals and brilliant yellow centers. For use in dried arrangements, try *Ammobium alatum* 'Grandiflorum', a larger, showier form with flowers ¼ to ½ inch across on 3-foot stems.
Cultural Information: Ammobium require full sun and dry, light soil. They are best propagated by seed sown in early spring.
Harvesting/Drying: The flowers will continue to open during the drying process, so it is best to harvest when the flowers are half opened. As they dry, they will expose their sunny yellow centers. Pick more flowers than you think you might need because they tend to shrink in the drying process. Hang the flowers to dry immediately. Truest color and best results are achieved by fast drying. The flower heads tend to droop after they are dried, so for use in arrangements, wire supports must be added.
Methods: Air-dry

Ammobium alatum

Anaphalis cinnamomea

(an-AFF-al-is sin-a-mo-MEE-a) **pearly everlasting,** perennial, easy. ○ ◐
Zones: 3 to 8
Height: 12 to 18 inches
Colors: White flowers, silvery foliage
Characteristics: The foliage of pearly everlasting is a delightful silvery gray color. The flowers, which bloom in late summer, resemble small white daisies. My favorite variety is 'Margaritacea', which has lovely gray foliage and a profusion of snow-white blooms in late summer.
Cultural Information: Live-everlasting, as it is sometimes called, is not fussy about soil, provided it is very well drained. To propagate from seed, start in a cold frame in early spring. Germination will occur in four to eight weeks at 55° to 60°F temperatures. Plant seedlings in the garden after all danger of frost. Space seedlings 12 inches apart. Because the seed is slow to germinate, it might

be best to purchase plants instead of starting from seed.
Harvesting/Drying: Harvest before the flowers are fully mature. Remove foliage from long stems and hang in a dry, well-ventilated place. *Anaphalis* will also dry nicely in an upright position. The delicate flower heads will need the support of a wire that you can add before or after drying. Make sure to dry them quickly so flowers will not mature and go to seed.
Methods: Air-dry, microwave

Anethum graveolens

(an-EE-thum) **dill,** easy, annual. ○
Height: 3 feet
Color: Pale yellow-green
Characteristics: Dill graces a garden with feathery foliage and lovely pale yellow, umbrella-shaped flowers. It has long wisps of bluish-green leaves with feathery tips, like fennel. Standing about 3 feet high, it should be planted toward the back of the garden border. In this position it can provide a wonderful backdrop for shorter plants. Try using this attractive herb in both your flower and vegetable gardens.
Cultural Information: Dill is a heavy feeder, so the soil should be rich and well drained. Prepare the soil in early spring by adding compost and well-rotted cow manure. It is best to direct sow seed in spring—dill does not like to be transplanted. Thin seedlings to 10 inches apart when the plants are 2 inches tall. For a continuous supply, plant seed every three weeks throughout the growing season. Choose the garden spot carefully, as dill tends to reseed, returning year after year. Germination will take 10 to 21 days, at temperatures of 65° F.
Harvesting/Drying: Harvest flower heads when they have been fully open for only about one day and before they have matured. Hang in a dry, warm, airy place out of sun, to retain color. The dried flower heads hold their distinctive scent after drying. Dill adds a light, airy look to dried arrangements.
Methods: Air-dry, silica, press, microwave

Aquilegia

(ak-wil-EE-jee-a) **columbine,** easy, perennial. ○ ◐
Zones: 4 to 8
Height: 2 feet
Colors: Blue, pinks, reds, yellows
Characteristics: Columbines are graceful, multicolored flowers adorned with long spurs. They nod upright above lacy, light green foliage. Each flower is made up of five petal-like sepals, set over five petals, which may be the same or a different color. Columbines are short-lived perennials, lasting about three years in the garden, but they freely self-sow when they like their home. These early summer perennials grace the garden in May and early June. After petals have dropped, they form attractive seed heads. These tiny crownlike green pods are held upright. There are several columbine varieties available including 'Harlequin' (an earlier blooming variety with large flowers) and 'McKana's Giant' (with large flowers in bright colors and bicolors). A more recent introduction, 'Nora Barlow', is an unusual, fully double flowering variety

Anethum gravelens

Aquilegia *'Harlequin Mix'*

with blooms of red, pink and green.
Cultural Information: Columbines are best grown in moist, well-drained soil. They will self-sow in favorable conditions. To propagate, sow seed in a protected area outdoors in midsummer or early fall. Cover new plants with a layer of winter mulch. Relocate to their permanent spot in the garden after danger of frost in spring. Space plants 12 to 24 inches apart.
Harvesting/Drying: The flowers of columbine can be dried successfully, but it is the seed heads that are most decorative. Harvest the seed heads in early summer, when they are a fresh green color. Water-dry them in an upright position. If you wish to dry the flowers, try the silica method and choose the yellow and blue varieties, which hold their true colors best. Columbine also has unusual foliage, which is useful in arrangements. To dry the foliage, try glycerine or the pressing method.
Methods: Air-dry (seed heads), silica, press (flowers)

Artemisia ludoviciana *'Silver King'*

Artemisia (ar-tem-IS-ia) **wormwood, southernwood,** easy, perennial. ○ ◐
Zones: 3 to 10
Height: Wormwood 2 to 4 feet, southernwood 5 feet
Color: Silver
Characteristics: Artemisia is grown for its aromatic, attractive foliage, not for its inconspicuous flowers that open during June and July. Wormwood, *A. absinthium,* is the best known of the artemisias. It is a wonderful ornamental herb, with attractive gray-green foliage. Wormwood grows on stalks that are covered with fine silky hair. 'Silver King', with graceful silvery gray spikes, is one of the best candidates for air-drying. It is a good substitute for German statice.
Cultural Information: Artemisias are not fussy. They prefer drier soil, but will thrive in any type soil, provided it is well drained. However, moisture is important during the growing season; additional water may be needed during periods of prolonged drought, especially during the first year. If you want more plants, make stem cuttings in spring or summer, or divide clumps in spring or fall. Space individual plants 12 to 18 inches apart when planting. Artemisia is generally pest- and disease-free.
Harvesting/Drying: The foliage of artemisia can be picked at any time during its growing season. Harvest on a dry day and hang to dry. The foliage is an attractive filler for arrange-

ıents. It also provides an in-eresting base material for vreaths and swags. The silvery olor of artemisia combines vell with many other dried ma-erials. Store after drying in lastic bags or airtight contain-ers to prevent it from reab-orbing moisture.

Methods: Air-dry, silica, press, nicrowave

Artemisia (ar-tem-IS-ia) **sweet Annie, sweet wormwood,** easy, annual. ○

Height: 4 to 6 feet

Colors: Silver-gray, green

Characteristics: Sweet Annie grows into a tall, pyramid-shaped plant that often reaches 6 feet. It has ferny, dark green foliage and a wonderful fra-grance.

Cultural Information: The an-nual sweet wormwood will thrive in most soils in a sunny spot provided it has adequate drainage.

Harvesting/Drying: Sweet Annie is grown for its soft green color, which blends well with any color. You will enjoy its lovely scent even after drying. Sweet Annie is a nice filler for dried arrangements and makes an ex-cellent base material for wreaths. Harvest Sweet Annie on a dry day before it has reached full maturity. Hang to air-dry.

Method: Air-dry

Asclepias tuberosa (a-SKLAY-pee-as tew-be-RO-sa) **butterfly weed,** easy, perennial. ○

Zones: 4 to 9

Height: 1½ feet

Color: Red-orange

Characteristics: Butterfly weed (so called because it attracts butterflies) is distinguished by coral buds that open to brilliant clusters of tiny rose-orange flowers. The flowers bloom in profusion from mid- to late summer. This heat- and drought-tolerant plant requires little attention, which is why it decorates roadsides and open woods so luxuriantly. The beauty of butterfly weed is that, unlike some other roadside plants, it is well behaved in the home garden. It produces showy seedpods in late summer. Collect these pods to use in dried arrangements.

Cultural Information: Butterfly weed prefers well-drained, sandy, or gravelly soils. Established plants can withstand drought due to their long taproot. It is this taproot, however, that makes butterfly weed difficult to transplant; it is best left undisturbed. Since these plants sprout late in the spring, mark where you plant them. The markers will remind you to not disturb the area. Seeds germinate in 28 to 42 days, preferring temperatures of 70° to 75°F. Seedlings can be started indoors for bloom the first year, or direct sown outdoors to bloom the following year.

Harvesting/Drying: Harvest seed heads in late autumn. If harvested late in the season, the seed heads will have turned a warm beige. They make handsome additions to natural autumn arrangements. Simply hang small bunches in a warm, dry spot.

Methods: Air-dry, press, microwave

Artemisia

Asclepias tuberosa

Astilbe

Astrantia major

Astilbe (a-STIL-bee) **garden spirea,** easy, perennial. ◐ ●
Zones: 4 to 8
Height: 12 to 14 inches dwarf form, 14 to 20 feet midheight, 3 to 4 feet tall
Colors: White, pale pink, peach, coral, red
Characteristics: The delicate flowering plumes of astilbe are a welcome addition to any garden. Few plants can rival astilbes for grace, charm and reliability. A wide range of heights and colors are now available. The tiny *Astilbe chinensis* 'Pumila', a handsome low-growing groundcover; grows to 12 inches and has soft lavender-pink plumes. *A. simplicifolia* 'Sprite' has cotton-candy pink plumes arching 16 inches above lacy, dark green foliage. 'Deutschland' sends up 18-inch white plumes that glow in semishady spots or at twilight. *A. arendsii*, false goat's beard, is the tallest one at 2 to 3 feet. Plant several different varieties to extend the bloom from early July into September. Astilbe plumes are good for cutting and drying.
Cultural Information: Astilbes prefer moist soil enriched with compost or leaf mold. Soil must be well drained in order for the plants to do well during the wet winter months. Heavy feeders, astilbes thrive on yearly spring applications of good organic mulch or dehydrated cow manure. Divide the clumps in autumn or spring about every three years. It is best to replenish the soil in the planting hole with peat moss, compost and a dusting of slow-release fertilizer before replanting. Because they have a tight root system, ample water is necessary, especially during dry periods. You can harvest all the flower stems in autumn or allow some to dry on the plant for added interest in the winter garden.
Harvesting/Drying: If you would like lovely soft pinks and whites for your arrangements, remember to harvest astilbes just before full bloom. Air-dry the pink- and rose-colored varieties; these usually hold their color best. The white plumes tend to turn cream-colored when dried. Try drying in a desiccant if you wish to keep the soft, natural colors. If, however, you are aiming for an autumn-colored arrangement, allow the flower heads to air-dry on the stalks and harvest in late summer. The earthy tones of the late summer astilbe combine perfectly with seedpods and the soft beige of hydrangea flowers. They make wonderful flowers for drying because their sturdy stems do not require wiring.
Methods: Air-dry, water-dry, silica, microwave

Astrantia major (as-TRAN-shia) **masterwort,** easy, perennial. ○ ◐
Zone: 6
Height: 2 feet
Color: Very pale pink with deeper pink veins
Characteristics: *Astrantia* has attractive lobed leaves and small, pinkish white umbelliferous flowers. Appearing June through August, the flowers tend to change in color as they mature. Lovely raylike bracts of deep rosy pink fade to pinkish white.
Cultural Information: To propagate by seed, you should sow the seed in autumn and allow it to overwinter before germination can take place. *Astrantia* can also be propagated by division in autumn. *Astrantia* thrives in sun or part shade and prefers moist soil.
Harvesting/Drying: *Astrantia*'s starlike flowers hold their color

best if silica dried. They can also be air-dried, but will fade slightly in color. Pick them throughout their growing cycle to have a wide range of color shading.
Methods: Air-dry, silica, press, microwave

Baby's breath; see ***Gypsophila***

Bachelor's button; see ***Centaurea***

Baptisia australis (bap-TIS-ee-a ow-STRAH-lis) **false indigo,** easy, perennial. ○
Zones: 3 to 9
Height: 3 to 4 feet
Colors: Blue, white, yellow, violet
Characteristics: Baptisia australis is best known for its indigo-blue flowers and blue-green foliage. The pea-shaped flowers grow along erect spikes and bloom in late spring and early summer. This long-lived plant grows to the size of a small shrub. It forms long black seedpods in late summer that remain on the plant until late fall. These interesting pods can be used in dried flower arrangements.
Cultural Information: Plant in well-drained soil in full sun. *Baptisia* can be grown in part shade but the flower production will be affected. It may need staking too prevent its branches from breaking.
Harvesting/Drying: Collect the showy seedpods in midsummer. They are easy to air-dry. It is best to dry them in an upright position to maintain their graceful curved stems. The pods can be sprayed with varnish to enhance their color.
Methods: Air-dry, silica, press (flowers)

Beauty-berry; see ***Callicarpa***

Bells of Ireland; see ***Moluccella***

Bergenia (ber-GEN-ee-uh) **bergenia,** moderate, perennial. ◐
Zones: 2 to 7
Height: 1 to 1½ feet
Colors: white, pink, red
Characteristics: The large evergreen leaves of bergenia provide interest in the garden throughout the year. The dense clusters of flowers that bloom in early spring are held high on strong stems. Harvest the flowers when they are in full bloom.
Cultural Information: Bergenia will grow in almost any soil. It will tolerate full sun in the North, but requires part sun in warmer southern areas. I grow it under a tree (filtered light) in my Zone 7 garden, and it does very well. Bergenia will fill in quickly and make a good ground cover for the front border.
Harvesting/Drying: Hang the flowers to dry in a warm spot. The colors of the flowers will deepen as they dry. The pink flowers, for example, will deepen to mauve. The stems are rather fleshy and difficult to dry, so it is best to clip the stem close to the flower head and use wire as the stem for arranging. The attractive mauve flower heads blend well with greens and white in arrangements.
Methods: Air-dry, silica, press

Baptisia australis

Bergenia cordifolia

Briza maxima

Black-eyed Susan; **see *Rudbeckia***

Butterfly weed; **see *Asclepias***

Briza maxima (BRY-za) **pearl grass, quaking grass,** easy, annual. ○
Height: 18 to 22 inches
Color: Green
Characteristics: The flowers of this ornamental grass produce unique heart-shaped spikelets. The decorative seed heads arch from strong, wiry stems. If you want beige seed heads, allow them to dry on the plant and then harvest them in late autumn.
Cultural Information: Quaking grass requires full sun and average soil. Like many of the ornamental grasses, it prefers poor soil. To propagate, sow the seed in early spring.
Harvesting/Drying: To maintain the green color when dried, harvest quaking grass early, when it is still green. Cut the stems before the seeds have matured. Dry in small bunches by hanging or standing upright in a warm, dark, dry location. Grasses are dry by nature and will be ready in four to five days.
Methods: Air-dry, water-dry

Bromus

***Bromus* spp.** (BRO-mus) **rye brome grass, rattle brome grass,** easy, annual. ○
Height: 2½ feet
Characteristics: Rye brome grass is an attractive, light green grass that develops purple seed spikes. It is used in dried arrangements as a filler.
Cultural Information: This grass prefers full sun and poor, dry soil. It is easy to propagate from seed. Rye brome will self-sow in milder climates.
Harvesting/Drying: Depending on the desired color, either collect seed heads when they are still green or wait and collect the mature seed heads when they have turned a lovely purple. Hang to air-dry.
Methods: Air-dry, water-dry

Calamintha nepetoides (kal-a-MIN-tha) **beautiful mint,** easy, half-hardy, perennial. ○
Zones: 7 to 9
Height: 18 to 20 inches
Color: Lilac
Characteristics: Unlike its cousins in the mint family, this attractive plant will not become invasive in the garden. It has pretty, thymelike, lavender-colored flowers that bloom from summer well into autumn. The flowers grow in clusters along the entire stem. Plant it next to a pathway or on a terrace, so its lovely minty fragrance can

Calamintha nepetoides

be close by. The strong, erect stems make it great for air-drying.
Cultural Information: Like most members of the mint family, calamintha prefers full sun and proper drainage. Although marginally hardy, it has survived many a winter in my Zone 7 garden.
Harvesting/Drying: Pick the flowers when they are just beginning to open. Dry them by hanging them in small bunches in a warm, dark spot. The beauty of this tiny treasure is as much the long-lasting minty fragrance as it is the lovely, delicate flowers.
Methods: Air-dry, silica

Callicarpa americana

(KAL-li-kar-pa) **American beauty-berry,** moderate, shrub. ○ ◐
Zones: 5 to 8
Height: 4 feet
Color: Purple berries
Characteristics: Beauty-berry is appropriately named. This rather nondescript shrub becomes the hit of the autumn garden when it produces its extraordinary deep purple berries. In the summer it has small bluish flowers.
Cultural Information: Beauty-berry does not require special soil or conditions and will bloom in both sun and part shade. It does, however, require a pruning to keep its shape and to encourage more fruit development.
Harvesting/Drying: Cut the branches in late autumn before the color starts to fade. Air-dry or water-dry for several weeks. Spray with shellac to further preserve.
Methods: Air-dry, silica

Beauty-berry

Carthamus tinctorius

(KAR-tham-us) **safflower,** moderate, annual. ○
Height: 1 to 3 feet
Color: Yellow opening to orange
Characteristics: Safflower is a colorful annual herb. Its thistlelike yellow florets open to a dark orange flower in late summer. The tight green buds are used for dried arrangements. Harvest the orange flowers in the late summer to be air-dried.
Cultural Information: Safflower likes a dry climate. Avoid excessive moisture, especially on leaves, as it may cause disease. Sow seeds in spring where they are to grow, ¼ inch deep. Thin seedlings to 4 to 6 inches apart.
Harvesting/Drying: Harvest the flowers for drying in late summer, when the maximum numbers of flowers are open, before they have overmatured. The green safflower buds are also an attractive addition to arrangements. If buds are desired, cut them before they mature in late summer. You can quickly check the readi-

Carthamus tinctorius

ness of air-dried flowers by snapping the dried stems. Store in an airtight container.
Methods: Air-dry, silica

Celosia cristata (se-LO-see-a) **cockscomb,** moderate, annual. ○
Height: 6 inches to 3 feet
Colors: Rose-pink, coral, salmon, purple, yellow
Characteristics: Once grown by settlers for medicinal purposes, cockscomb is now a favorite flower for drying and cutting. Few flowers can provide as wonderful a display of color in late summer. Cockscomb is reliable and quick to grow, and makes a terrific accent plant in the garden. The crested flowers resemble a rooster's comb, thus its common name. A mainstay of any dry flower garden, celosias provide color and texture to dried arrangements. *Celosia plumosa* (the plumed cockscomb) is extremely showy. These well-branched plants have silky, feathery plumes from midsummer to frost. Try some of the new varieties such as the All-American winner 'Apricot Brandy' or the showy new dwarf variety 'New Look', which has intense scarlet plumes and deep bronze foliage. My favorite dried flower in 1993 was a new introduction named 'Pink Flamingo'. It dried beautifully and had a showy, pale pink, tassel-like flower.
Cultural Information: Plant celosia in full sun in average, well-drained soil. Celosia are heat-loving plants that tolerate drought. It is best to start the seed in a greenhouse because the plants are sensitive to cold temperatures and root disturbances. Germination takes from 7 to 10 days if temperatures are constant between 65° and 75°F. After germination, they require a cooler growing temperature of 60°F.
Harvesting/Drying: Pick the flowers right before they are in full bloom. Foliage can be left on the stems during the drying process. Hang small bunches to air-dry. Make sure they are fully dry by snapping a few stems to check for crispness. After drying, store the flowers away from moisture and bright sunlight. Celosia dry beautifully but they will lose some of their natural vibrant colors.
Methods: Air-dry, silica

Celosia cristata

Centaurea cyanus (sent-OW-ree-a see-AH-nus) **bachelor's button, cornflower** easy, annual. ○
Height: 1 to 2½ feet
Colors: White, pale blue, dark blue, maroon
Characteristics: Bachelor's button is an old-fashioned flower that has enjoyed popularity for good reason. They made fashionable boutonnieres for gentlemen years ago. Bachelor's buttons come in several heights. The low border plants 'Jubilee Gem' and 'Polka Dot Mixed' are just 12 to 15 inches in height. Dusty miller is usually grown as an annual in colder northern climates. This tender perennial over winters in my Zone 7 garden and will return to produce tiny clusters of yellow flowers.
Cultural Information: Sow seed in early spring in cold winter areas, and in late summer or fall where winters are mild. Bachelor's buttons are very adaptable and grow in poor, sandy or average soil. Fertilizer is not necessary unless the soil is unusually poor. For a continuous supply of flowers, deadhead daily. Because of their weak stems, the taller varieties need staking to prevent sprawling.
Harvesting/Drying: Bachelor's buttons air-dry easily. Pick buds and immature flowers daily; it is best to collect the flowers before they have become too mature. Drying mature flower heads is more difficult because their colors fade and the flowers are very fragile. Wire weak stems for support before drying. To air-dry, stick the stems through wire racks with the flower facing up. If they are dried in silica gel they tend to hold their

Centaurea cyanus

Chrysanthemum parthenium

Cineraria maritima

true form better and are not as brittle and difficult to handle when arranging. Save the dropped petals of the more mature flowers to use in potpourri mix.
Methods: Air-dry, silica, press, microwave

Chinese lantern; see ***Physalis***

Chrysanthemum parthenium (kris-ANTH-em-um par-THEE-nee-om) **feverfew,** moderate, half-hardy, annual. ○
Height: 3 feet
Color: White
Characteristics: Feverfew is a member of the daisy family. The clusters of small, white, daisylike flowers with brilliant yellow centers are often confused with chamomile flowers. The green foliage is finely indented and often strong-scented. It has long been a favorite in many cottage gardens. The flowers are useful in dried bouquets as a filler flower.
Cultural Information: Grow feverfew in ordinary, well-drained soil and full sun. Start seed indoors in flats in late winter and plant outdoors after danger of frost. Once established, feverfew will self-sow freely and bloom throughout the summer months.
Harvesting/Drying: Cut feverfew when in full flower and remove the foliage. Hang to air-dry.
Methods: Air-dry, silica, microwave

Cineraria maritima (sin-ne-RAH-ee-a ma-ri-TEE-ma) **silver-dust,** easy, annual. ○
Height: 12 inches
Color: Grayish white
Characteristics: The lacy, silvery foliage of dusty miller makes an interesting contrast in flower borders, rock gardens and containers. The foliage complements and enhances other more colorful annuals such as blue ageratum. *Cineraria maritima* 'Silverdust' grows 9 inches in height and has a finely cut, silvery white foliage with a velvety texture. *Chrysanthemum ptarmicaeflorum* 'Silver Lace', a less-common form, is a more compact plant that grows 7 inches tall and has a more finely cut silvery gray foliage.
Cultural Information: Dusty miller prefers ordinary, well-drained or poor, sandy soil. It thrives in areas that are hot and dry. This hardy annual is long lasting and survives a light frost.
Harvesting/Drying: Dusty miller is wonderful for air-drying. It makes a lovely filler in dried arrangements. Harvest the mature foliage of dusty miller any time during the growing season (just

Clematis *'Duchess of Albany'*

Consolida orientalis

make sure it is dry and free of any excess moisture). Hang small bunches in a warm, dry, dark spot. Hanging will cause the foliage to curl slightly. I have had some success in keeping the foliage pliable by drying the foliage in glycerine. Another way to retain the natural shape is to press the foliage between pages of a book just as you would press ferns and other flat foliage plants.
Methods: Air-dry, press, glycerine

Clematis (KLEM-at-is) **clematis,** moderate, perennial. ○
Zones: 2 to 7
Height: 4 to 20 feet
Colors: White, pale pink, dark pink, red, lavender, pale blue, dark blue, purple, yellow
Characteristics: These vines are an important part of the garden because they provide vertical interest. Most produce fluffy seed heads in later summer and early autumn that are attractive in dried arrangements. The hybrid varieties with large-flowered heads are particularly popular. The flowers can be pressed and preserved in silica gel.
Cultural Information: Clematis are not particular about soil; however, they do appreciate a healthy dose of lime sprinkled around their base yearly. They like to reach for the sun while their feet remain in the coolness of shade. You can help by placing a stone or pieces of a broken clay pot over their roots. Just be careful not to touch the stem.
Harvesting/Drying: Cut the fluffy seed heads on a dry day and hang to dry. The seed heads of clematis differ in size greatly and can add interest to any dried arrangement. Some of the larger flowering hybrids will work especially well if pressed or preserved in silica gel.
Methods: Air-dry, silica, glycerine, press

Cockscomb; see ***Celosia***

Columbine; see ***Aquilegia***

Coneflower; see ***Echinacea***

Consolida orientalis (kon-SO-li-da) **larkspur,** easy, annual. ○ ◐
Height: 1 to 2 feet
Colors: White, blue, pink
Characteristics: Larkspur is a graceful flower that is indispensable to the summer border. Densely flowered spikes provide masses of color in the border or along a fence or wall. It is one annual that every dried flower arranger will find essential. Its color range and height make wonderful additions to any arrangement.

For a more informal feeling, grow larkspur in a wildflower meadow or on a sunny slope. The single or double florets and fine, light green foliage provide splendid color from late spring into summer. 'Giant Imperial Mixed' from Burpee blooms in shades of blue, pink and white and dries beautifully. It is an outstanding cut flower and easy to air-dry. It retains its bright colors all winter. Don't confuse larkspur with delphinium, which is a tender perennial in many zones. Delphinium has a thicker flower stalk and tight clusters of

ırger flowers that make drying ıore of a challenge.
'ultural Information: Start the eeds indoors eight weeks be- ɔre the last frost. I stratify eed for one to two weeks to ncourage germination. Be- ause larkspur do not like root isturbance, start them in peat ots that can later be planted irectly into the garden. You an also direct sow the seed 'here plants are to grow. Thin eedlings to 6 inches apart. ome stalking might be eeded. In southern areas, lant six to seven weeks before rst expected frost. Southern ardeners should have success 'intering over larkspur, but 'armer summer temperatures horten their bloom time consid- rably. In southern gardens, the est blooms occur in the cooler pring and early summer months.
Iarvesting/Drying: Pick the owers early (when half of the looms are unopened). Do not llow the flowers to become too ıature or they will not dry as 'ell. Hang to air-dry immedi- tely after harvesting. Store dry arkspur stems in a flat box 'ith tissue paper between lay- rs. The dried flowers tend to e brittle so take precautions 'hen handling. To prevent lamage to stems, spritz lightly 'ith water before arranging.
Iethods: Silica, press, microwave

'ornflower; see ***Centaurea***

'raspedia globosa (crass-'EE-dee-a glo-BO-sa) **drum stick,** asy, annual/biennial. ○
Ieight: 3 feet
'olor: Yellow
'haracteristics: Craspedia flow- rs are brilliant yellow globular balls, 1 inch across. Flower heads appear in late summer and continue well into autumn. The flowers are held firmly upright on straight, strong, 3-foot stems, which makes them look like drum sticks. They are wonderful for dried arrangements.
Cultural Information: Sow the seeds in early spring indoors or in a coldframe. Plant the seedlings out in the garden after all danger of frost. Space the seedlings 6 to 8 inches apart. Craspedia may need staking to ensure straight stems for drying. Plant next to Russian sage or one of the blue salvias for a striking color combination.
Harvesting/Drying: Pick the flowers just when they have fully opened. Hang dry quickly, in a warm, dry spot so that the stems dry completely and remain straight.
Methods: Air-dry, silica, microwave

Daffodil; see ***Narcissus***

Dahlia (DAH-lee-a) **dahlia,** moderate, tender tuber. ○ ◐
Height: dwarf 12 inches; giant 5 feet
Colors: White, pink, blue, yellow, orange, multicolored
Characteristics: Dahlias come in a variety of sizes, shapes and foliage colors. The showy flowers bloom from midsummer to frost. Dahlia flowers range in size from large dinner-plate size to tiny pompons less than 2 inches across. Single, double, cactus, pompon, peony and quilled flowers types are available. Foliage comes in medium to dark green and deep burgundy. There are dwarf varieties with large 2- to 3-inch flowers for the front of the border, medium-height varieties for the middle, and tall varieties foı the back of the border. The tall varieties can also be grown as a floral hedge. Some continue blooming late in the fall after light frost and right up

Craspedia globosa *'Gold Stick'*

Dahlia

Daucus carota

to heavy frost. In warmer climates dahlias will overwinter.

The smaller double or pompon dahlia varieties make wonderful dried flowers. Try Burpee's 'Pompon Dahlias Mixed', which bloom in white, pale pink, yellow, orange and red.

Cultural Information: Plant the tubers after danger of frost in well-drained soil. Space dwarf plants 12 inches apart and tall varieties 3 feet apart. Remember to add stakes for taller varieties at planting time. Dahlias can also be propagated from seed, cuttings or root division. In colder northern climates, after leaves are blackened by frost, dig up the tubers that have formed over the summer and store them in dry peat moss. Check these tubers often to make sure they have not rotted from dampness. Tubers in warmer areas can stay in the ground, but mulch them heavily with salt hay or straw to protect from colder winter temperatures. In areas with mild winters it is not necessary to dig and store. A layer of winter protection will always help protect tubers from light frost.

Harvesting/Drying: Pick flowers at the height of bloom or petals will drop. Hang them up to air-dry immediately. Small pompons and single daisylike dahlias both work well. Two of my favorite dahlias are 'Duet', which is a rich red color, and 'Snowstorm', which is a clean white color. Both of these hold their colors after drying. Avoid the large dinner plate–size dahlias; they are too difficult to dry successfully. Using silica is the best method of drying dahlias if you want to maintain the natural color and shape. It is important that the silica powder surrounds the petals completely. Many of the smaller pompon type dahlias can be air-dried by placing them on a wire rack in a drying room. Air-drying dahlias is easy and fast (approximately two weeks), but some fading of colors is to be expected. Most of the larger flowered dahlias will need to be reinforced with wire before drying.

Methods: Silica, microwave

Daucus carota (DAW-kus karōta) **Queen Anne's lace,** easy, annual. ○

Height: 1½ to 2 feet

Color: Creamy white

Characteristics: Queen Anne's lace has lovely lacy, creamy white flowers that bloom in late summer. It grows alongside roads and in meadows where it has naturalized. In fact, in many states it is illegal to sell the seed because it has escaped from gardens and is now so prolific that it crowds out American native flowers. It is perfect for both fresh and dried arrangements and is easily air-dried.

Cultural Information: Queen Anne's lace, which is usually found growing in sunny, open areas, has few requirements. It does not require fertile soil, but does best in soil that is well drained. It will self-sow vigorously if flower heads are allowed to go to seed.

Harvesting/Drying: Collect the flower heads when they have just opened, before they begin to curl and turn an off-white color. The flowers can be air-dried by putting the stems through a wire rack. With this method the flower heads tend to shrink up and curl a bit. The best way to preserve the flowers is to place the heads face up in a box and surround and cover them with desiccant. For another interesting look, allow some of the flower heads to mature on the stems. They will curl up and form lacy balls.

Methods: Air-dry, silica, press

Delphinium (del-FIN-ee-um) **delphinium,** challenging, perennial. ○ ◐

Zones: 3 to 8

Height: dwarf, 14 to 25 inches; tall, 6 feet

Colors: Blue, purple, lavender, white

Characteristics: Delphiniums are strikingly beautiful plants—the glory of a June garden. The best-known varieties flower on 6-foot spikes. Showy single flowers or double-rosette blooms contrast with the dark green broad to finely cut leaves. In my Zone 7 garden, delphiniums are short lived and unreliable. I find it best to replant them yearly, treating them like annuals. *D. elatum* 'Giant Pacific' is a majestic plant that grows u

)elphinium elatum, *'Fantasia Mix'*

) 6 feet tall. It blooms in hades of pink, blue and violet. 'or drying purposes, the horter varieties are a bit easier) work with. Burpee-bred *D. latum* 'Fantasia' is a semidw-rf plant (only 27 inches high) vith flower spikes as large and howy as tall delphiniums, and t needs no staking. It is easy o grow from seed, and blooms he first season when started arly indoors. 'Fantasia' flowers n a color mixture of white, lav-nder, and shades of blue. For n even smaller variety, try *D. randiflorum* 'Blue-Elf', a com-)act, 14-inch plant with very inely divided foliage, and in-ense midblue florets. Caution hould be taken because all lelphinium foliage is poisonous f eaten.

'ultural Information: Delphini-ms are fussy about soil. They equire a light soil, rich in or-ganic matter with good drainage. The plants are heavy feeders nd require several applications of 5-10-5 fertilizer throughout he season. It is important to add ime to acid soil because del-)hiniums prefer an alkaline soil. Delphiniums require cool nights, rich soil and a constant supply of moisture. Only under these soil and weather conditions will they be a permanent addition to your plantings.

Winter mulch, applied after the ground has frozen, may be needed for cooler areas. Start seed indoors in cold climates in March or April, to set out seedlings in June. You may have some bloom the first season but you will have many more in subsequent years.

Plant in spring, after danger of frost, 1½ to 3 feet apart. Tall varieties will require staking for support. After the first blush of bloom in June, cut back and they may bloom again in the fall. They will require division after their third year. In mild-winter areas, start seed in flats in July through August and set out transplants in October. They will bloom the following spring.

Harvesting/Drying: Delphinium are larger and meaty in texture, they are more difficult to air-dry than larkspur. Pick flowers when only about half of the blooms are opened. A later cutting, when the flowers are fully opened, will provide more color and interest. Don't allow the flowers to mature or they will not dry well. Success in drying delphinium depends on speed; the faster you dry them the more successful you will be. Silica gel will have better results than air drying. Individual flowers also press nicely and retain their vibrant colors.

Methods: Air-dry, silica, press, microwave

Devil-in-the-bush; see ***Nigella***

Dill; see ***Anthemum***

Drum stick; see ***Craspedia***

Dusty miller; see ***Centaurea***

Echinacea (ek-in-AY-sea)
coneflower, easy, perennial.
○ ◐

Zones: 3 to 9
Height: 2 to 3 feet
Colors: Pink, white
Characteristics: Coneflower is a wonderful addition to any garden. It is a sturdy plant with showy flower heads 3 to 4 inches across. The flowers resemble black-eyed Susan, but have reflexed petals, and bloom

Echinacea

in pink and white. The foliage, 3 to 4 inches long, is dark green and coarse in texture. *Echinacea* is an American native and is lovely when grown in an informal or woodland garden setting.
Cultural Information: Echinacea will grow in an ordinary soil but prefers soil enriched with compost to help it tolerate heat and drought. Grow individual plants from seed. Prevent overcrowding by dividing every three years. Space plants 18 inches apart and enrich the soil before replanting.
Harvesting/Drying: For dried arrangements allow the flower heads to dry naturally on the plant before harvesting. Seed heads are also interesting in dried arrangements.
Methods: Air-dry, silica

Echinops (EK-in-ops) **globe thistle,** moderate, perennial. ○
Zones: 3 to 8
Height: 4 to 5 feet

Echinops

Colors: Violet to steel blue
Characteristics: Globe thistle is a rugged perennial with sharp, spiky round blooms. The attractive blue flowers provide interesting texture and form both to the garden and to flower arrangements. As the flowers mature, they turn a silvery blue color. *Echinops* provides outstanding, long-lasting flowers and foliage for use in fresh and dried arrangements.
Cultural Information: Echinops grows best in well-drained soil of average fertility. Space plants 18 to 24 inches apart. Plant from the middle to the back of the border to conceal the rather tattered lower foliage. Propagate by sowing seed in late spring or by root division in early spring. For best flower production it is necessary to divide every three to four years. They may be difficult to divide, however, because roots are deep and dense.
Harvesting/Drying: It is critical to harvest *echinops* when the florets are just about to break bud, before the lovely blue color fades and before the flowers are fully opened. If allowed to become too mature, they will be extremely delicate and rather unattractive in appearance. Carefully remove the prickly foliage before drying. The strong stems do not require wiring. These wonderful blue spherelike flowers are interesting in arrangements.
Methods: Air-dry, silica

Eryngium (e-RINJ-ium) **sea holly,** moderate, perennial. ○
Zone: 5
Height: 2 to 3 feet
Color: Steel blue
Characteristics: Sea holly has showy, silvery gray foliage and steely blue flowers. Two popular species are *Eryngium giganteum* (a biennial with large flower heads) and *E. alpinum* (with a smaller, deeper blue flower head). Both are good candidates for air-drying. The flowers look like those of *echinops,* but they are smaller and less fragile.
Cultural Information: Propagate by sowing seed. Allow for a period of dormancy; the germination is slow. Once established, *Eryngium* is a sturdy heat and drought-tolerant plant. It is best grown in full sun and average soil with good drainage.
Harvesting/Drying: Harvest the fully developed flower heads before their blue color begins to fade. They are not as delicate as *echinops* and can be either hung to air-dry or dried in an upright position. The strong stems of *Eryngium* do not require wire after air-drying.
Methods: Air-dry, silica, microwave

Everlasting; see ***Ammobium***

Everlasting flower; see ***Xeranthemum***

False indigo; see ***Baptisia***

Feverfew; see ***Chrysanthemum parthenium***

Floss flower; see ***Ageratum***

Garden spirea; see ***Astilbe***

Globe amaranth; see ***Gomphrena***

Globe thistle; see ***Echinops***

Golden ageratum; see ***Lonas***

[G]oldenrod; see ***Solidago***

[G]omphrena globosa ([g]om-FREE-na glo-BO-sa) **globe [a]maranth,** moderate, half-[h]ardy annual. ○
[H]eight: 12 to 24 inches
[C]olors: White, pink, purple, or-[a]nge, red, rose, reddish purple
[C]haracteristics: Gomphrena has [a]n attractive, cloverlike flower [h]ead. The flowers appear [th]roughout the summer in [w]hite, pink, rose, reddish pur-[p]le and orange. *Gomphrena* [l]ooks good in cutting gardens, [fo]rmal borders and containers. [F]or container growing, plant [th]e dwarf variety 'Buddy', [w]hich grows to 9 inches. Pots [o]f *Gomphrena* can be brought [in]to a greenhouse as cold [w]eather approaches. The flow-[e]rs will continue for a long [ti]me, after which you can cut [b]ack and start fertilizing. When [w]eather permits, you can bring [th]em outside to start reblooming. [T]he flowers are useful in both [fr]esh and dried arrangements.
[C]ultural Information: Gom-[p]hrena will grow in average, [w]ell-drained soil. This hardy [a]nnual tolerates both drought [a]nd heat.
[H]arvesting/Drying: To maintain [s]trong color, it is best to har-[v]est *Gomphrena* flowers when [th]ey are fully opened. *Gom-[p]hrena* can be picked late in [th]e season, but some color fad-[in]g may occur. Hang to air-dry.
[M]ethod: Air-dry

[G]ypsophila panicu-[l]ata (jip-SOf-i-la pan-ik-yew-LAH-[h]) **baby's breath,** moderate, [p]erennial. ○
[Z]ones: 3 to 10
[H]eight: 36 to 48 inches
Colors: White, pink
Characteristics: Baby's breath is tiny white clouds of flowers on strong branching stems. The plant adds an airy effect to both the summer garden and winter dried arrangements. The flowers appear in midsummer and continue to bloom until early fall. Try growing the large double-flowered variety 'Bristol Fairy'. 'Early Snowball' is an early blooming variety with small, double flowers. *Gypsophila* is also available in the annual form *G. elegans,* which has lance-shaped foliage and pink to white flowers. Another annual, 'Covent Garden White', has clusters of large white flowers. Both of these annuals can be easily air-dried and used in arrangements. The flowers tend to darken into an off-white color after drying. This antique-white color is preferred for certain projects.
Cultural Information: Gypsophila does best in well-drained, alkaline soil in full sunlight. A generous handful of lime sprinkled yearly in a circle around the base of the plant should keep the soil alkaline. The roots of baby's breath are deep and need a lighter soil through which they can penetrate. Propagate by sowing seed in early spring, or taking cuttings in late spring. Plant baby's breath 36 inches apart. Like most perennials, it requires division after three years. Annual *Gypsophila, G. elegans,* is best propagated by direct sowing seeds in early spring.
Harvesting/Drying: Cut flowers before they are fully opened, but past the bud stage. In late autumn, cut the entire plant

Gomphrena globosa

Gypsophila paniculata

Gramineae Grass Family

Grasses come in both annual and perennial forms. There are more than 400 different species of grasses and they all make wonderful dried material. Some of the best candidates for drying are the common forms found growing wild alongside the roads and highways.

Grasses can be harvested in early summer when their color is a soft gray-green, or in late summer when it's a golden bronze. To dry, place grasses upright in a container. The upright position will help them keep their soft, natural look after drying.

Helichrysum bracteatum

Tall Helichrysum

back close to the ground. Hang upside down to dry in a warm, dark room. The stems become brittle after drying, so it is often necessary to spritz them with water a short time before arranging. This will help keep the stems pliable and they'll be less likely to break. Another way to preserve their stem pliability is by using the glycerine method of drying. Store in boxes with tissue paper between layers. The strong stems do not require wire for support.
Methods: Air-dry, water-dry, silica

Helichrysum bracteatum (hee-li-KRY-sum brak-tee-AH-tum) **strawflower,** easy, half-hardy annual. ○
Height: 12 to 15 inches for dwarf varieties, 3 feet for tall variety
Colors: Yellow, orange, salmon, bronze, crimson, pink, white
Characteristics: This old-fashioned everlasting garden flower makes a bright addition to any winter bouquet. The strawflower is one of the best-known everlasting flowers. The flowers come in a wide range of colors, including yellow, pink, crimson, white and bronze. This reliable annual will reward the gardener with an abundance of showy flowers from midsummer until heavy frost. *Helichrysum* are also attractive container plants.
Cultural Information: Helichrysum will grow in average, well-drained soil. Their biggest enemy is heavy rain and poor drainage, which will rot their stems. Start seed indoors in March to assure a full season of growth and harvest. The seed should germinate in 15 days. Plant outdoors after danger frost. Space the plants 1 inches apart.
Harvesting/Drying: Don't mak the mistake of harvesting th flowers of *Helichrysum* too lat It is best to cut before th flowers become too mature an their yellow centers are visibl For interest and variety, tr cutting some in the bud stag You should remove all foliag before hanging to dry. I recom mend you wire the stems be cause they tend to become wea and are unable to support th flower heads. Try tucking re strawflowers into garlands or e ergreen wreaths for festive an long-lived holiday displays.
Method: Air-dry

Helipterum roseu (sometimes referred to a ***Acrochinium roseum***) (hell-IP-ter-um) **immortell flower,** easy, half-hardy an nual. ○
Height: 18 to 24 inches
Colors: White with yellow cen ter, pink with yellow cente red with black center.
Characteristics: Helipterum ha a strong stiff stem with gray green foliage and large, daisy like flowers. It is just one the approximately 60 species dried flowers that originated i South Africa. The flower head usually solitary, are 2 inche wide. They are commonl available in white or pink wi yellow centers although som more unusual ones are red wit a black center. Flowers bloo from June to September.
Cultural Information: Sow see in early April, ⅛ inch deep Maintain temperatures of 55 to 65°F to ensure proper germ

ation. Transplant outdoors after ll danger of frost. Thin to 8 nches apart. Don't forget to arden off plants that have been tarted indoors before planting utside. A well-drained soil, rich n humus but slightly acid is referable. These plants do not olerate soil that has been limed. Plants flower about eight weeks fter the seed is sown. Plants end to have sparse-looking foiage so it is best to grow them n rows in a cutting garden or vith fuller plants in front to over their lower stems.
Iarvesting/Drying: Harvest the lowers on a dry day. Collect lowers that have just begun to pen or while in the bud stage. Iarvesting flowers in several tages of development creates nore natural looking arrangenents. Remove the foliage and ecure bunches with rubber ands. Hang in a dark, dry, vell-ventilated place.
Method: Air-dry

Iollyhock; see ***Alcea***

Iop; see ***Humulus***

Humulus (HEW-mew-lus) **hop,** moderate, perennial. ○
Zones: 3 to 9
Height: 20 to 25 feet
Color: Greenish yellow
Characteristics: Humulus lupuus is a vigorous climber that grows to 20 feet each summer. Hops are dioecious, which neans that male and female lowers grow on separate plants. The female flowers produce atractive green pinecone-like lowers. These flowers produce he essential oils and acids that are used to brew beer. They are also interesting additions to winter arrangements. The variety 'Aurea', which has yellow foliage, is usually grown as an ornamental.
Cultural Information: Start seed indoors early or outdoors after danger of frost. Or propagate from cuttings in the spring. Plant hops in an open area with good air circulation, which will help prevent mildew diseases. Provide a strong support and rich soil and hops will happily scramble past the height of their original support in no time. Apply 5-10-5 fertilizer in early spring.
Harvesting/Drying: Hops add interest to swags and over-door decorations. Collect the fully developed flowers from late summer until early autumn. Don't harvest before they have matured or they will shrivel during the drying process. They can be air-dried by hanging or in an upright position. You can also make a fresh arrangement and simply allow it to dry naturally. Handle hops carefully after drying as they tend to be rather brittle. You will notice a subtle scent for several weeks after harvesting.
Methods: Air-dry, water-dry, microwave

Helipterum roseum

Hydrangea (hy-DRAN-jia) **hydrangea,** moderate, deciduous shrub. ○ ◐
Zones: Varies—3 to 9
Height: 30 feet
Colors: White, pink, lilac, blue
Characteristics: Hydrangea is a beautiful old-fashioned garden shrub. It was widely used in Victorian times. Two forms are especially useful for dry flower arranging. *Hydrangea paniculata* ("peegee") is a wood shrub

Hydrangea paniculata

that produces attractive large white flowers. The flowers turn a warm pink color on the plants and finally green and brown. Peegee hydrangeas are hardy in Zones 3 to 8. The other hydrangea frequently used in dried flower arrangements is *Hydrangea macrophylla* ("bigleaf hydrangea"). This produces flowers that range in color from pink to deep blue depending on the soil. *Hydrangea macrophylla* will produce blue to purple flowers if grown in acid soil and pink flowers in alkaline soil. As the hydrangea flowers develop and mature on the plant they will lose their original color and turn a silvery beige. Marginal in Zone 6, it is quite reliable from Zone 7 southward.

Cultural Information: Hydrangeas require rich, porous soil. They need good drainage and ample watering especially during hot dry periods. Plant them in areas that provide afternoon shade. Fast growing, they can reach up to 10 feet. Prune to control their size. For bigger flower heads, prune out a larger number of stems. This will encourage the remaining ones to produce larger heads.

Harvesting/Drying: The flower heads can be picked throughout the season if they are to be dried in desiccant. If they are to be air-dried, it is best to wait until they feel leathery to the touch before harvesting. Another option is to allow the flower heads to dry naturally on the plant, where they will develop a silvery beige color. One of the best species for drying this way is the peegee hydrangea. The flower heads of the peegee hydrangea are quite long and can be broken apart into many tiny clusters for use in arrangements.

Methods: Air-dry, water-dry, microwave

Immortelle flower; see ***Helipterum***

Lady's mantle; see ***Alchemilla***

Lamb's ear; see ***Stachys***

Larkspur; see ***Consolida***

Lavandula (lav-AN-dew-la)
lavender, moderately difficult, perennial. ○

Zones: *L. angustifolia,* 6 to 9 (provide protection in Zone 6); *L. dentata,* 9 to 10; *L. officinalis,* 5 to 10; *L. stoechas,* 8 to 10

Height: 12 to 18 inches for French, 12 to 36 inches for English

Colors: Blue, lavender, white

Characteristics: This shrubby herb, a favorite in herb and perennial gardens, has decorativ silver-gray foliage and fragran lavender flowers that bloom from July through August. Lavender forms dwarf-flowerin hedges and is attractive linin a walk or edging a perennia garden. The fragrant flower and foliage are the mainstay c sachets and potpourri and ar equally at home in dried o fresh arrangements. Native t the Mediterranean, lavende has naturalized in the souther United States. There are som 28 different species. The mos popular varieties are *Lavandula angustifolia,* found i every old-fashioned herb garden, with tiny clusters of blu to purple flowers; fringed lavender (*L. dentata*), with green fernlike foliage and blue flowers; English lavender (*L. officinalis*), with needlelik silvery-gray foliage and dee purple or white flowers. Hard in Zones 5 to 10, munstea dwarf (*L. munstead* 'Hidcote'

Lavandula

rows to a height of 18 inches nd has silvery foliage and lavnder flowers almost the hole summer.

ultural Information: Lavender refers average, well-drained oil that is slightly alkaline. oil that is too rich will rob the lants of essential oils that prouce fragrance. To propagate, ake cuttings in the summer rom half-ripened shoots or sow eeds. If the plants are sown rom seed, lavender will flower n the second year. But if the eeds are sown early indoors, here is a good chance of flowrs in the first season. The foiage stays on the plant all vinter. In early spring, cutting ack the foliage to a few inches rom the ground is an enjoyable ask. You'll carry fragrance vith you all day from having andled the foliage. Cut the lead branches back in the pring after the new growth beins. Spanish and fringed lavnder can be grown indoors as otted plants in the winter and utdoors in the summer.

Iarvesting/Drying: For potourri, sachets and scented pilows, harvest in late summer vhen the flowers can easily be eparated from stems. Strip the lowers when they are in full loom or as they open. Dry hem in an airy, shaded place n trays or screens. When dryng lavender for flower arrangenents, cut lavender early efore the buds open. Hang to ir-dry. Handle the dried lavnder gently because it beomes brittle when dried. The romatic fragrance of lavender vill last for a long time after lrying.

Methods: Air-dry, silica

Limonium (ly-MO-nium) **sea lavender,** easy, perennial. ○

Zone: 3

Height: 2½ feet

Color: Mauve flowers

Characteristics: Native American sea lavender is a perennial that grows along coastal areas and in salt marches. It develops soft lavender clouds of flowers that appear in late summer. Sea lavender is a protected plant and should not be picked from the wild, but several garden species such as Carolina sea lavender (*Limonium carolinianum*) are available to home gardeners. Their dried flowers are useful in dried arrangements.

Cultural Information: Sea lavender prefers full sun, but will take some shade. It thrives in moist soil and is usually found growing alongside the shoreline in salt water. The garden varieties can be grown in average, well-drained soil in full sun.

Harvesting/Drying: Harvest *L. carolinianum* when the flowers have opened and before the centers start to discolor. Sea lavender air-dries easily and has a more informal look than *L. sinuatum.* It is very useful as a filler or background material for wreaths and arrangements.

Methods: Air-dry, water-dry

Limonium sinuatum (ly-MO-nium sin-ew-AH-tum) **statice,** moderate, annual. ○

Height: 2½ feet

Colors: Blue, yellow, rose, white, orange-yellow, salmon-pink, pink-carmine

Characteristics: This old-time favorite is one of the most versatile annuals to grow for drying. It comes in a wide range of colors, including white, yellow, pink, rose, blue, lavender and apricot. Blooms appear from midsummer to fall. The stems are strong, the foliage rough and leathery. The clusters of tiny, papery, pastel-colored flowers add charm and interest to any dried arrangement. Statice is probably the most durable of all dried materials. It can withstand handling and poor storage conditions better than most other dried materials.

Cultural Information: The biggest enemy of statice is overly moist soil. It adapts to heat and drought, salt spray and any type of soil except heavy clay.

Limonium sinuatum

Limonium latifolia

Limonium sinuatum

African daisy

To propagate, sow the seed indoors in early spring or late winter. Germination should take approximately 10 to 20 days at temperatures of 65° F. Harden off and plant outdoors after all danger of frost. In southern or milder climates, direct sow the seed in late spring, after danger of frost.
Harvesting/Drying: Harvest the statice when it is dry and the blooms are approximately three-quarters open. Remove the foliage before air-drying. Save all the tiny flower petals to use in potpourri or other small projects. Statice will become very brittle after air-drying. Preserving it in a glycerine solution will make it less brittle and easier to work with. To retain color it is best to protect dried statice from direct sunlight.
Method: Air-dry

Limonium suworowii (ly-MO-nium) **poker statice,** moderate, half-hardy annual. ○
Height: 18 inches
Color: Pink
Characteristics: Limonium suworowii is an outstanding addition to borders. Striking pink flowers cover gracefully curved spikes. This unique plant has a twisted appearance, which adds interest both to gardens and to arrangements.
Cultural Information: Sow the seeds in full sun in average, well-drained soil.
Harvesting/Drying: Statice flowers appear mid- to late summer. Cut bunches before all the blossoms have opened fully. Hang to air-dry. The strong stems don't need the additional support o wire.
Methods: Air-dry, water-dry silica

Lonas inodora (LOW-na in-o-DO-ra) **African daisy golden ageratum,** easy, hard annual. ○
Height: 12 to 18 inches
Color: Yellow
Characteristics: The Africa daisy's clusters of bright yello flowers bloom in late summe The flowers appear on strong branching stems that do not re quire wiring. The flowers re semble those of *Achille filipendulina,* but are muc smaller. This hardy annual is nc affected by a light frost and wi bloom well into autumn. Plan *Lonas inodora* in borders fo long periods of interest an color. They combine well wit annual blue salvia or in front o late-blooming purple asters.
Cultural Information: Lonas inodora will grow in almost an soil, provided it has goo drainage. In warm climates, di rect sow the seed in April. I climates with late spring, so the seed indoors in March, ½ inch deep, at temperatures o 55° F. Plant outside after dan ger of frost. Space the seedling 12 inches apart.
Harvesting/Drying: Harvest th flowers of the African daisy jus before they are fully opened Remove the foliage and secur with rubber bands in bunche of no more than five heads Hang the bunches in a dark dry, well-ventilated spot.
Methods: Air-dry, silica, microwave

ove-in-a-mist; see ***Nigella***

ove-lies-bleeding; see ***Ama-anthus***

unaria annua (loo-NAY-AN-ew) **money plant, Pope's noney, honesty,** easy, bien-ial or annual. ○
leight: 3 feet
olors: Violet or white, silvery eedpods
haracteristics: The money lant is an old-fashioned gar-en plant grown for its showy eedpods. It is best grown in n informal setting or meadow. he small clusters of flowers re violet or white in color. A tandard of Victorian European arlors, this lovely plant was ot grown in America until the 930s. It produces circular eedpods that dry into translu-ent silvery discs. These pods re extremely decorative and seful in dried arrangements.
ultural Information: The noney plant is easily grown rom direct sown seed. In early ummer, biennial plants need o be seeded where they will lower the following summer.
Harvesting/Drying: This plant needs very little drying time. Pick the silvery white seedpods when dry and papery. Remove the outer brownish discs (the outer seed cover) by gently rubbing. A lovely silvery disc will be uncovered. Air-dry in an upright or hanging position until stems are dry. Handle gently as they tend to become very brittle.
Methods: Air-dry, microwave

Marigold; see ***Tagetes***

Lunaria annua

Masterwort; see ***Astrantia***

Moluccella (mo-lew-SEEL-a) **bells of Ireland,** moderate, annual. ○
Height: 2 to 3 feet
Color: Apple-green
Characteristics: Bells of Ireland produce pale green shell-like bracts that resemble small bells. Tucked deeply into each bract are tiny, white, fragrant flowers. It is grown primarily for its lovely ornamental 2- to 3-foot spikes covered with the apple-green bracts. These spikes can be used in fresh or dried arrangements.
Cultural Information: Bells of Ireland require good drainage and average soil. Seed germination is slow and unreliable; it is often necessary to chill seed in the refrigerator, then

Moluccella

soak it overnight in warm water to soften and remove the hard seed coat. Do not cover seeds because they need light to germinate.
Harvesting/Drying: The tiny white flowers appear in late summer. Harvest when the bells have become firm to the touch (about 7 to 10 days after they appear). Remove the lower foliage before drying. Tie small bunches together to air-dry. The bells will turn straw color when dry. Salvage any fallen bells for potpourri or tiny arrangements. Glycerine can also be used to dry.
Methods: Air-dry, water-dry, glycerine

Money plant; see ***Lunaria***

Narcissus (nar-SIS-us) **daffodil,** easy, bulb. ○ ◐
Zones: 4 to 10
Height: Varies depending on the variety from 4 to 24 inches
Colors: White, yellow, orange or any combination of the three
Characteristics: A large and varied family, daffodils are among the most self-sufficient of bulbs. There is much confusion over the family's name. For all practical purposes, the names daffodil and *Narcissus* are interchangeable; daffodil is the English common name for the Latin classification of *Narcissus.*

I know of one grower with 4,000 different daffodils and there are more than three times that number of registered varieties. If well planned, a naturalized daffodil planting, including early, mid- and late-season varieties, can last two to three months or longer. A turn-of-the-century garden writer said, "One could never have enough of such a rare gold."
Cultural Information: Daffodils prefer light, well-drained soil, rich in humus. Plant the bulbs two to three times as deep as their diameter. Work the soil a few inches deeper than is necessary to plant, in order to give the bulbs a prepared bed into which they'll send their delicate roots. Normal moisture usually provided by spring and fall rains is all they require. Some tolerate wet soil conditions better than others. Divide the bulbs when the plants produce nothing but foliage and replant in organically enhanced soil. Some varieties ('February Gold', for example) increase more rapidly than others.

Narcissus

Nigella damascena

Harvesting/Drying: Pick the flowers in late morning after the dew has dried. Drying daffodils is for the patient person. Their stems are meaty and almost refuse to dry, so it is best to simply remove the flowers and leave the foliage to rejuvenate the bulb. Silica gel is the only method I know to successfully dry them. They tend to fade slightly in color but will retain a natural shape if hung separately after drying. I have tried air-drying and found that they lose their lovely yellow color and turn a dull beige.
Methods: Air-dry, silica, press, microwave

Paonia *'Bridal Gown'*

Nigella damascena (ny-JELL-a dam-a-SKAY-na) **love-in-a-mist, devil-in-the-bush,** moderately easy, annual. ○
Height: Dwarf, 6 inches; standard variety, 12 inches
Colors: White, pink, purple, blue, lavender
Characteristics: Love-in-a-mist is an old-fashioned favorite. It produces airy blue or white flowers. But like many dried flowers, its true beauty is in the decorative, pod-shaped seed heads, which are surrounded by frilly foliage. The pods of the blue flowers have showy, pinkish red veins. If left to mature into seedpods, they will self-sow freely about the garden.
Harvesting/Drying: For dried pods, harvest love-in-a-mist after the flower petals have dropped. Wait until the pods have fully developed, but pick before the pods lose their lovely pink-veined coloring. If left to dry naturally on the plant, they will fade and shrivel. For dried flower heads, cut them early and dry quickly before the petals drop.
Methods: Air-dry and silica (seed heads), press (flower heads)

Oriental poppy; see ***Papaver***

Paeonia (PEE-o-nia) **peony,** moderate, perennial. ○
Zones: 3 to 8
Height: 2 to 4 feet
Colors: White, pink, crimson, red, coral, bicolors
Characteristics: Peonies are one of the first flowers of May. They have large showy flowers, and some varieties are highly fragrant. These showy plants will last a lifetime in the garden if given the proper setting.
Cultural Information: Peonies prefer full sun and well-drained soil. Plant about 2 to 3 feet apart. Cover the eyes with 1½ inches of soil and mulch in areas of extreme winters. They don't perform well in warm climates such as the Southwest and Southeast regions of the United States because they need some winter cold for dormancy.
Harvesting/Drying: It is important to pick peonies before they are exposed to extreme temperatures. If drying with silica, it is best to choose the single or semidouble varieties. You will find that these varieties are easier to surround completely with silica gel. If you want to try your hand at air-drying, select the large double varieties. They will shrink a bit in size but still hold much of their natural color and beauty. The foliage of tree peonies can also be preserved by pressing.
Methods: Air-dry, silica, microwave

Papaver orientale

Papaver orientale (pa-PAY-ver o-ree-en-TAH-lee) **Oriental poppy,** moderate, perennial. ○ ◐
Zones: 3 to 7
Height: 16 inches to 4 feet
Colors: Scarlet, orange, white, rose, crimson, salmon
Characteristics: Poppies are another dried flower grown for their highly decorative pods. The perennial Oriental poppies produce large, showy pods. Many annual poppies also produce attractive smaller pods. Allow a few annual seedpods to ripen on the plants. This will ensure a continuous supply of poppies next year.
Cultural Information: Perennial poppies are a bit more demanding in their growing requirements than annual poppies. They prefer areas with cool summer temperatures and are short-lived in warm-winter areas. They do not appreciate being transplanted. It will take about two growing seasons for them to become established. Mulch in summer to keep their roots cooler. Annual poppies will grow in average, well-drained soil. Sow the seed directly into the garden in early spring or late winter.
Harvesting/Drying: The flowers of poppies are almost impossible to dry successfully, but the seedpods are easy to dry and very decorative. The pods are green in the early stage and mature into an attractive beige. Don't pick them too early because they need to dry on the plant before harvesting. Harvest both annual and perennial poppy pods before damp weather discolors them. Hang small bunches to air-dry.
Method: Air-dry (seed heads)

Paper moon; see ***Scabiosa***

Pearl grass; see ***Briza***

Pearly everlasting; see ***Anaphalis***

Peony; see ***Paeonia***

Physalis alkekengi (FISS-a-lis al-ke-KEN-jee-ee) **Chinese lantern,** easy, perennial. ○
Zones: 3 to 10

Physalis alkekengi

Height: 2 feet
Color: Orange
Characteristics: Chinese lanterns are showy autumn plants grown for their brilliant orange, lanternlike pods. *Physalis* is actually a member of the nightshade family.
Cultural Information: Chinese lantern prefers a sunny spot. It is not fussy about soil, but choose its growing spot carefully because it can become invasive. Once established it sends out underground runners. Plants may remain undisturbed indefinitely. If clumps become overcrowded, root cuttings or clump divisions may be made in the fall or spring. All will provide "lanterns" during the first growing season.
Harvesting/Drying: Harvest stems in late summer when pods have completely turned a warm orange color. Remove the foliage and hang to air-dry. Stems can also be dried in an upright position in a warm, dark, dry spot.
Methods: Air-dry, water-dry

Poker statice; see ***Limonium***

Pope's money; see ***Lunaria***

Quaking grass; see ***Briza***

Queen Anne's lace; see ***Daucus***

Rattle brome grass; see ***Bromus***

Rosa (RO-sa) **rose,** moderate, perennial. ○
Zones: 4 to 10
Height: 2 to 5 feet
Colors: White, pink, coral, red, yellow, bicolors
Characteristics: The Greeks called the rose "queen of flowers" and indeed it is. The rose, which comes in a wide range of colors and sizes, is the most popular flower grown around the world, a universal symbol of love and beauty. Some of the older varieties are grown not only for their beauty but also for medicinal and culinary purposes. Many types of garden roses can be used for drying. Don't limit your choices to tea roses; many shrub roses and climbers dry wonderfully well, also. I love the look of our 'Fairy' hedge rose, which features many tiny pink roses growing in clusters. They air-dry well, but tend to shrink and curl a little. The effect is lovely and makes a welcome addition to any dried arrangement. A well-placed rose can add life and elegance to a dried arrangement. Fasten some dried roses onto a simple swag or wreath for instant glamour.
Cultural Information: Roses prefer full sun, good drainage, and soil rich in organic matter. They also prefer good air circulation, which helps prevent mildew and disease on the foliage. Roses need large amounts of water (3 inches weekly) but must have fast-draining soil. Feed roses with a slow-release fertilizer in early spring and after the first flush of bloom. A topdressing of well-rotted manure in late autumn will add nutrients to the soil. Organic matter is always beneficial to roses, but remember to check the pH, which should be at or close to 7. Add lime after application of manure to ensure a proper pH. Old roses are very disease resistant so there is no need to spray these roses with chemi-

Rosa *'Betty Prior'*

cals. However, it is important to keep the garden clean and free of faded petals and fallen leaves. Garden litter is a tempting place for insects and pests to breed. If insects are a problem, try sprinkling onion water (cool water in which onion has been boiled) or onion mulch (chopped onion greens) around the base of the plants. Shrub roses need little pruning and look best left to their natural shape. Prune once a year before the buds appear, in early spring or late winter. Simply cut out dead or old canes and cut existing stems back by one-third. Roses can be propagated from cuttings, but it is wiser to purchase your plants from catalogs and garden centers.

Harvesting/Drying: Your success with drying roses depends on the methods of drying and the colors of the roses. Hang drying works quite well with most roses; rosebuds, for example, air-dry very well. However, mature roses hold their shape and color best when dried quickly using a silica gel. Red and dark pink roses will dry close to their natural color. Yellow, pale pink and white roses tend to turn a beige color at the base of their petals when air-dried. White roses also take on an antique cream color after drying. The faster the drying time, the better the natural color will be retained. The time of harvest depends on the effect you wish to achieve. If you want to dry roses in full flower, pick them in late morning after the dew has dried and before the heat of midday. If rosebuds are your choice, harvest them in late morning after dew is dry and before they begin to open from the warmth of the sun. To air-dry buds, simply cut the stems at the desired length and hang them upside down in your drying room. To air-dry more open roses, pick ones that have just opened but are not yet matured. Remove the thorns from the rose stems and save the foliage. Secure in small bunches (being careful not to crush the individual flowers). Hang to air-dry in a warm, dark room. The stems and flowers of the dried roses will become very brittle, so use caution when arranging them. If some petals do come loose, glue them back carefully. Save all fallen petals to use in potpourri.

Methods: Air-dry, silica, press, microwave (tea roses and buds)

Rudbeckia fulgida
'Goldsturm Strain'

Rose; see ***Rosa***

Rudbeckia spp. (rood-BEK-ia) **black-eyed Susan,** easy, perennial. ○

Zones: 3 to 9

Height: 2 to 4 feet

Colors: Yellow, orange, red

Characteristics: Black-eyed Susan is a showy, daisylike native American perennial often found in natural meadows and along roadsides. It provides wonderful garden color all summer long. Black-eyed Susans make long-lasting cut flowers. Their range of petal colors includes yellow, orange, red and bronze. When the petals fall off, they leave a dark, attractive cone-shaped center. This dark core is excellent for use in dried arrangements. *Rudbeckia hirta* 'Gloriosa Daisy' has profuse displays of large blooms up to 5 inches across on 3-foot stems.

Cultural Information: Plant black-eyed Susan 2 feet apart in average, well-drained soil. Divide the clumps in spring or autumn every four years. Dividing will ensure a more robust production of blooms. These tolerant plants will grow in poor soil and can withstand the extreme heat of summer.

Harvesting/Drying: You can harvest black-eyed Susan at any time during its development. Just decide what size center you want to dry. Remove the petals and hang up the centers to dry. If you prefer, simply allow the flowers to mature on the stems and harvest later. The individual petals can be pressed and then reattached to the core with glue before mounting on a board.

Methods: Air-dry, microwave

Rye brome grass; see ***Bromus***

Safflower; see ***Carthamus***

Salvia (SAL-via) **salvia, sage,** easy, annual, perennial. ○

Zones: 4 to 9

Height: 1 to 4 feet

Colors: Red, deep purple, blue, pink, bicolor

Characteristics: There are many types of saliva (both annual and perennial), and I have found that most air-dry beautifully. They bloom in a wide range of colors including palest pink, fire engine red, deep purple and bicolor.

One of my favorite annual sal-

Salvia farinacea

brush sage and 'Purple Majesty' before collecting into small bunches. Tie into small bunches to avoid crushing. Hang up to air-dry.
Methods: Air-dry, water-dry, silica, press, microwave

Sand flower; see ***Ammobium***

Scabiosa atropurpurea

(skab-ee-O-sa aht-ro-pur-PEWR-ee-a)
scabious, starflower, paper moon, easy, hardy annual. ○
Height: 24 inches
Color: Lavender
Characteristics: Starflower has soft lavender flowers arranged as if on a pincushion. It also has lovely, greenish-beige star-like pistils that remain after the petals fall. The stems are solid and strong enough to support the starflower heads.
Cultural Information: Direct sow seed in spring after last expected frost. Thin seedlings 12 inches apart or sow the seed the same distance apart. For an

vias for drying is *Salvia farinacea,* which has beautiful spikes of white or blue flowers. Mexican brush sage and 'Purple Majesty' are also grown as annuals in my Zone 7 garden and are the highlight of the late summer garden. No dried flower arranger would be without clary sage (*S. sclarea*), with its brightly colored bracts ranging from greenish white to purple. Common sage (*S. officinalis*), which is usually grown as an herb, has attractive and aromatic foliage that can be dried and used in arrangements. Meadow sage (*S. pitcheri*), a dark blue sage that blooms in late summer, is one of my favorite perennial salvias. I have found through experimentation that most salvias hold their color, shape and fragrance long after drying.
Cultural Information: Salvias generally prefer full sun and average, well-drained soil. Most perennial salvias will not return if grown in areas of poor drainage.
Harvesting/Drying: Cut salvia when bracts feel slightly papery. Remove the foliage of *Salvia farinacea,* Mexican

Scabiosa *'Giant Imperial'*

early start, sow seed indoors in peat pots. Plant outdoors after danger of frost, and space 12 inches apart.
Harvesting/Drying: Cut flower heads before they are fully mature. Secure in small bunches. Be careful not to crush the individual flowers. The dried blossoms are very delicate and need special care when handling. Starflower blooms dry very quickly.
Methods: Air-dry, silica, press, microwave

Scabious; see ***Scabiosa***

Sea holly; see ***Eryngium***

Sedum *'Autumn Joy'*

Sedum (SEE-dum) **stonecrop, sedum,** easy, perennial. ○
Zones: 3 to 9
Height: 3 inches to 2 feet
Colors: Yellow, red, pink, white
Characteristics: Sedum is a succulent plant that thrives in full sun. It boasts clusters of showy flowers from late summer into fall. *Sedum purpureum* 'Autumn Joy' makes a fine addition to any garden because it brings year-'round interest to the border. If allowed to dry naturally on the plant, the flower stalks will turn an attractive rust-red color. And in winter, they will support a layer of snow.
Cultural Information: Sedums are not fussy about their soil, but they insist on well-drained conditions. They are tolerant of drought. Sow the seed in late summer or mid-spring at 65° F or take stem cuttings any time of year.
Harvesting/Drying: Pick the flower heads of sedum just before they have fully opened. If you harvest early in the flower's development, you can retain some of the pinkish-red color. Sedum flowers picked in late summer and early autumn will have a beige color. To dry sedum, remove all foliage and tie in small bunches to air-dry. For even better results try the silica or microwave methods.
Methods: Air-dry, silica, microwave

Solidago (sol-i-DAY-go) **goldenrod,** easy, perennial. ○ ◐
Zones: 3 to 7
Height: 1 to 4 feet
Color: Yellow
Characteristics: Goldenrod is considered a weed by most Americans, but it is grown widely in European gardens. The more than 125 species of *Solidago* have woody stems and numerous yellow flower heads on terminal clusters. Tiny (¼ inch) disklike flower heads grace this plant. Goldenrod is not the culprit of hay fever, as some believe. However, it often grows alongside ragweed, which does cause hay fever. Goldenrod's pollen is too heavy to be blown by the wind, so it falls to the ground.
Cultural Information: Goldenrod is not fussy about soil or drainage and will often grow in areas that are constantly moist. It spreads rapidly and self-sows, which is the cause of its weedlike reputation.
Harvesting/Drying: Cut the flowers in autumn before their brilliant yellow color fades. Hang to air-dry. Goldenrod looks lovely used in natural arrangements.
Methods: Air-dry, water-dry, microwave

Southernwood; see ***Artemisia***

Stachys (STA-kis) **lamb's ears,** easy, perennial herb. ○ ◐
Zones: 4 to 9
Height: 1 to 1½ feet
Colors: Pink flowers, silvery-gray foliage
Characteristics: Stachys byzantina is one of the finest of the silver-leafed plants. It forms a dense mat of woolly leaves with a spread of 1 foot. Lamb's ears is named for its soft, downy

leaves that resemble the shape and velvety texture of a baby lamb's ear. The tiny pink flowers appear in early summer. Once *Stachys* was used to bandage the wounds of soldiers. Today it is used as an ornamental plant for its interesting silvery foliage.
Cultural Information: Lamb's ears like full sun and well-drained soil. It is best to propagate by root division in early spring or fall or to buy started plants. Seeds sown in spring take two years to develop into mature plants. Space 12 inches apart. This hardy herb will spread quickly, forming a tight, matlike groundcover. It will need to be divided every two to three years to prevent overcrowding.
Harvesting/Drying: Cut the flower stalks of lamb's ears before the flowers mature. Hang bunches to air-dry. The silvery foliage, which retains its beauty even after air-drying, can also be dried or pressed. The dried foliage is a lovely base material for a wreath. You can use a press to dry the silvery foliage or simply lay the leaves on a flat surface. Remember to turn them often.
Methods: Air-dry, press (foliage)

Stachys byzantina

Starflower; see ***Scabiosa***

Statice; see ***Limonium***

Stonecrop; see ***Sedum***

Strawflower; see ***Helichrysum***

Sweet Annie; see ***Artemisia***

Sweet wormwood; see ***Artemeisia***

Tagetes (ta-GAY-teez) **marigold,** very easy, annual. ○
Height: 10 to 36 inches
Colors: White, yellow, orange, red
Characteristics: Native American flowers, marigolds are one of the most reliable annuals in the summer border. They come in a wide range of colors and sizes, from the tiny French marigold to the tall Burpee 'Marvel Hybrid' series with large 4-inch flowers on 24-inch stems.
Cultural Information: Marigolds are virtually carefree. They will thrive in heat and

Tagetes erecta *'First Lady'*

drought, and poor or sandy soil. The seed for marigolds can be direct sown or started six to eight weeks before the last expected spring frost. They are easy to transplant. Many are quick to bloom, and resistant to disease. They make long-lasting cut flowers.
Harvesting/Drying: Cut the flowers when they are still fresh. The smaller varieties and the single forms are best dried in a desiccant. Many of the large-flowering varieties are easy to air-dry.
Methods: Air-dry, silica, microwave

Tanacetum (tan-ass-EE-tum) **tansy,** easy, perennial. ○
Zones: 4 to 10
Height: 2 to 4 feet
Color: Yellow
Characteristics: Tansy is an attractive addition to your garden. Native to Europe, it has naturalized in North America and is often seen growing along roadsides. The pungent, fern-like leaves were once used as stewing herb, but are now used as an insect repellent. This reliable plant grows about 2 to 4 feet tall with an equal spread. It should be planted at the back of the border and staked to prevent wind damage. The attractive blooms are clusters of button-shaped, yellow flowers that bloom in mid- to late summer. Isolate tansy because its aggressive creeping roots can become invasive.
Cultural Information: Tansy will grow in any garden soil, but prefers moist, loamy soil. Sow seeds in early spring or late fall, or propagate new plants by root division in early spring. Space the plants 12 to 24 inches apart.
Harvesting/Drying: Pick flowers at the peak of their color, before they have fully opened. Remove foliage and hang to air-dry. The flowers will fade a bit but they still make a sunny addition to dried arrangements.
Methods: Air-dry, silica, microwave

Tanacetum officinale

Tansy; see ***Tanacetum***

Tulip; see ***Tulipa***

Tulipa (TEW-lip-a) **tulip,** difficult, bulb. ○ ◐
Zones: 3 to 7
Height: 6 to 24 inches
Colors: Yellow, pink, red, white, purple, bicolor
Characteristics: Everyone knows the tulip family for its gorgeous garden stars blooming in late spring. There are many different types of tulips besides the popular cup-shaped hybrids. Explore "peony-flowered," lily-flowered, fringed, "parrot," and the many double-flowered varieties. If properly planned, a garden can have tulips in continual bloom for two months or more.
Cultural Information: Well-drained, light, rich humus is

the best soil for tulips. They are also fond of lime. It is helpful to scatter Holland Bulb Booster on top of soil at the rate recommended by the manufacturer. Water it in at planting time and every fall thereafter. Water very well to start the roots growing in fall. Replace tulips every year if you want the same number of bulbs, as in a formal planting.
Harvesting/Drying: Tulip drying is for the courageous. Silica gel is the only successful method. Carefully place the tulip face up into a paper cup slightly larger than the diameter of a cup-shaped tulip. Gently pour the silica to encircle and cover the tulip. For double tulips shaped like peonies or roses, follow the instructions for drying peonies and roses in silica gel.
Methods: Air-dry, press, silica, microwave

Wide-leaf sea-lavender; see ***Limonium***

Winged everlasting; see ***Anaphalis***

Wormwood; see ***Artemisia***

Xeranthemum (zee-RAN-them-um) **everlasting flower, immortelle,** easy, hardy annual. ○
Height: 18 to 24 inches
Colors: White, pink, rose
Characteristics: Everlasting flowers, which may be single or double, range in color from white to deep rose. Their stems are sturdy and have pale green leaves with a downy texture. Everlasting flowers are very useful in dried arrangements, wreaths and swags. They hold their color and shape for a long time.
Cultural Information: Xeranthemum likes full sun and will grow in most well-drained garden soils. Sow the seed where they are to bloom in late spring. Be sure to wait for the soil to warm to about 60° F. Germination should take approximately 20 days.
Harvesting/Drying: Flowers will retain their color in the garden for a long time. Harvest the flowers at various stages of development from half open to fully opened. Be sure to pick them before their colors begin to fade or become damaged by

Tulips

Xeranthemum annum

Zinnia *'Pink Splendor Hybrid'*

dampness. *Xeranthemum* is in the category of everlasting flowers, which means that it is naturally dry and free of moisture in its petals. After you harvest the flowers, hang them to dry.
Method: Air-dry

Yarrow; see ***Achillea***

Zinnia (ZIN-nia) **zinnia,** moderate, half-hardy annual. ○
Height: 6 inches to 2½ feet
Colors: White, pink, red, yellow, orange
Characteristics: Zinnias, which come in many radiant colors, are the glory of the summer garden. The flowers range in size from 2 inches to 6 inches. Some have ruffled petals and others are open like daisies. They bloom in a few weeks from seed and withstand hot dry weather. Zinnias make wonderful cut flowers and also dry nicely when placed in silica gel.
Cultural Information: Zinnias like well-drained garden soil enriched with rotted compost. They are prone to mildew, so it is best to water at the base rather than overhead. You can also buy one of the new mildew-resistant varieties such as Burpee's 'Pinwheel' Series, which comes in wonderful colors. To encourage bushy plants, remember to pinch the blossoms back. The more you cut, the more zinnias will produce. My favorites are the dahlia-like double-flowered zinnias such as 'Burpee's Big Tetra Mixed' and 'Giant Flowered Mix', which dry beautifully.
Harvesting/Drying: Collect flowers to be dried at their peak of bloom, and before they have started to fade in color. Check to make sure the flowers you pick are not discolored by mildew.
Methods: Air-dry, microwave

6

PESTS AND DISEASES

Some of the flowers that you will be growing for the purpose of drying have a natural ability to protect themselves against pests and disease. Herbs such as tansy, feverfew and marigold have a built-in defense system (a pungent fragrance), which guards them against harmful insects. Many of the other perennials and annuals grown for the purpose of drying will not be affected by pests if provided with proper growing conditions. However, even in the best of gardens sometimes there are problems; early detection is your best defense. Check your garden often for problems.

In recent years a new approach to pest and disease control has become popular. This program, Integrated Pest Management (or IPM), stresses the importance of providing proper growing conditions and diagnosing early signs of possible trouble. If a pest or disease problem does occur, IPM suggests several totally organic remedies. Here are some basic good gardening practices to help you start your IPM program.

RULES FOR A HEALTHY GARDEN

1. Your best defense against disease and troublesome insects is a garden that has healthy, well-prepared soil. Soil that is healthy and weed- and disease-free will produce strong plants that can better ward off attacks of insects and disease. (To learn more about soil preparation, see page 17.)
2. Keep the garden free of garden litter and weeds. Litter is a breeding place for insects. Clean up spent flower heads except those you will want to collect for their ornamental seed heads.
3. Never water your garden in the heat of midday or after the sun goes down. Midday watering is wasteful because of evaporation; watering after dark encourages invasions of slugs, snails and mildew. Use a soaker hose to help conserve water and prevent water damage on foliage.
4. A thin layer of mulch will help preserve moisture and prevent weeds. Avoid thick layers of mulch that will become hiding places for garden pests.
5. Not all insects are pests. Learn to distinguish the good insects from the harmful ones. Introduce beneficial insects such as ladybugs, green lacewings and praying mantises into your garden. These tiny garden soldiers can consume several times their weight in harmful insects each day. They can be shipped to your home from Burpee and other environmentally concerned garden catalog companies.
6. Nature has a way of telling you what works and what doesn't work. If a particular plant just does not seem to thrive in your garden, try growing a different plant in that spot. You can do your best to ensure a plant's success, but nature makes the final decision. I give a specific flower two chances before replacing it with another variety. With all of the wonderful varieties to choose from, why waste space and time on a poor performer?

Aphids

Aphids have long, slender beaks that pierce plant tissue and suck out the plant's juices. They can also introduce infections and spread disease from one plant to another. Although aphids are quite small, they usually appear in large groups, which makes them easy to detect. They have soft, pear-shaped, multicolored bodies. Apply a strong spray of water or an organic insecticide at two-day intervals because eggs will continue to hatch for several days.

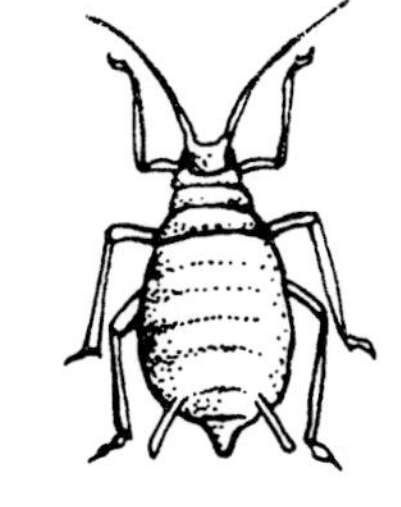

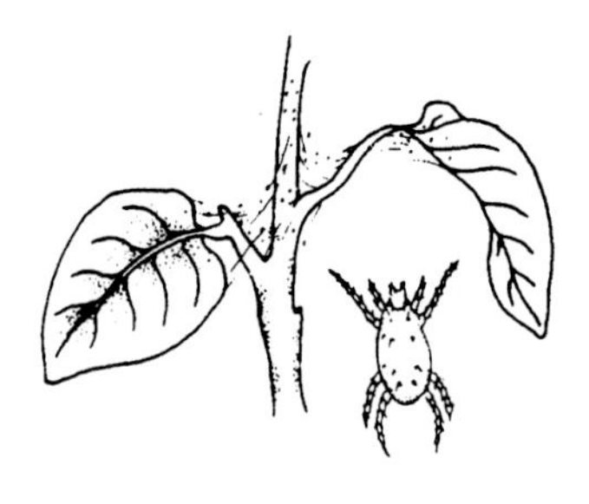

Spider mites

Spider mites appear as tiny red spots on the underside of leaves. Like aphids, they pierce leaves and suck out the plant's juices, which causes the leaves to yellow, wither and ultimately drop off. Wash affected plants with a strong spray of water or use a spray of an organic insecticide. Introduce ladybugs into your garden; they are a natural enemy of spider mites.

Beetles

A number of kinds of beetles attack perennials, but the Japanese beetle is the most common. These beetles feed on the foliage of plants and spread diseases from one plant to another. The best way to prevent an infestation of Japanese beetles is to treat them while they're in the grub stage, living in the soil and feeding on the roots of grass. Several organic products (Ringer's Grub Attack, for example) kill by infecting grubs with milky spore, a disease caused by *bacillus popilliae,* a natural ingredient. A single application continues to kill grubs for many years.

Slugs and Snails

These little creatures are easy to spot. Snails are encased in a shell and slugs are out of the shell. They are usually brown, black, gray, tan or yellow. Both snails and slugs usually feed after the sun has gone down or on dark, overcast days. They leave a telltale trail of slime letting you know where they have been. The best method of prevention is to spread a circle of wood ashes, lime or diatomaceous soil (coarse earth made from silica-rich diatom shells) around the base of susceptible plants or around the entire perimeter of the garden. These products are rough in texture so when slugs crawls over them, they are torn open and soon die. Although very effective, these products must be reapplied after every rain. Another effective trap is to set bowls of beer in the ground; snails and slugs will crawl into the bowls and drown.

DISEASES

Powdery Mildew

Powdery mildew appears as a white felty covering on the foliage or leaves. It is caused by surface parasites that thrive in humid, but not rainy, weather. Powdery mildew is common on phlox, chrysanthemums, zinnia and roses. It will eventually kill the affected plant.

Botrytis

Another common disease is botrytis (gray mold blight), which is caused by damp, humid conditions. The best way to control both powdery mildew and botrytis is to provide good air circulation, a clean garden and proper watering.

Most of the pests and diseases I've discussed can be controlled by using a few preventative techniques. It is essential to check your garden regularly for signs of insects or disease. If trouble does occur, quick action is important. Today we are fortunate to have many organic products that help control pests and diseases. Safer's Garden Fungicide, for example, can rid your plants of botrytis if used early enough. If the infestation or disease is impossible to control you will need to dispose of the diseased plant. Place the affected plant in the garbage, not on the compost pile where it will reinfect future plants.

7

GARDENERS' MOST-ASKED QUESTIONS

The first Burpee catalog was mailed in 1876, and the catalogs have been coming ever since, offering gardeners seeds, flowering plants, fruits, shrubs and trees as well as advice on better gardening. From the earliest years, Burpee has received letters from customers describing their gardens and asking for help with the problems they encounter. Here are the most frequently asked questions concerning dried flowers.

Q. How do I dry flowers?
A. The simplest method is to cut them just before peak bloom, remove foliage, tie a few stems together and hang them upside down in a dry, dark place with good air circulation for a couple of weeks.

Q. Can any flower be dried?
A. No. Many flowers and seedpods shatter or wither after cutting. However, about 80 percent of all flowers will have some degree of success, depending on the method of drying. Silica gel, while the most complicated, is the method that will give the greatest success to the greatest variety of flowers.

Q. Do some flowers lose their color when they are dried?
A. Yes. Achillea, bells of Ireland and celosia are just a few of the many flowers that fade in color when air-dried. White flowers tend to turn a beige color. This color change can be rather romantic. White roses, for example, acquire an antique-white color after drying. The silica gel method is the best way to preserve color.

Q. Why do my flowers bend after I dry them?
A. Perhaps you are not hanging them upside down after picking them, or you may be picking them too late. If flowers are dried standing in a vase, the weight of the flowers will bend the stems as they dry.

Q. What are the easiest annual flowers to grow for drying?
A. The flowers known as everlastings: *Gomphrena,* strawflower, statice, winged everlastings, *Xeranthemum* and starflower.

Q. What are the easiest perennial flowers to grow for drying?
A. *Achillea,* perennial baby's breath, perennial ornamental grasses, sedum 'Autumn Joy', and astilbe.

Q. What are the easiest seedpods for drying?
A. Chinese lantern, money plant, love-in-a-mist and black-eyed Susans.

Q. Which shrubs produce flowers or berries for drying?
A. Hydrangea (especially the blue lace cap and peegee kinds), *Clethra* species, lilac, beauty-berry and *Cotinus* (smoke tree) produce interesting dried flowers.

Q. Which herbs produce flowers that are good for drying?
A. Lavender is the most popular herb for drying. The aromatic foliage of many herbs, such as rosemary and thyme, can be used in potpourri or in bouquets.

Q. Which flowers for drying grow in shade?
A. Honesty, Chinese lantern, astilbe, hydrangea and clethra.

Q. How long do "everlastings" really last?
A. They can last for years, although their color may fade in time, especially if they are in a sunny location.

Q. What is the best way to preserve the color of everlastings?
A. Be sure not to pick them after their peak of bloom and try to keep them out of direct sunlight. Some flowers, such as bells of Ireland, achillea and celosia, fade naturally.

Q. Can I pick flowers fresh and let them dry when the water in the vase evaporates?
A. This works with some dried flowers with stiff stems, such as baby's breath, statice and hydrangea. Others need to hang upside down to dry to ensure straight stems.

Q. What are some good ornamental grasses for drying?
A. Pampas grass, *Briza maxima* or *Briza media* (quaking grass) and *Deschampsia* (tufted hair grass) are attractive in dried arrangements.

Q. What foliage dries well?
A. The aromatic foliage of many herbs, such as rosemary, sage and artemisia, are good for drying for potpourri or arrangements.

Q. Do roses make good dried flowers? They never dry well for me.
A. Tiny rosebuds are easy to air-dry by hanging in a warm dry spot. The open roses are more difficult to dry, but they respond well to silica gel drying. Rose petals or small rosebuds are also popular ingredients in potpourri. Cut the flowers in the morning and gently pull off the petals. Spread the petals on a drying rack and allow them to dry for a couple of days, or spread them on a cookie sheet and put them in the oven for a couple of hours at about 110° F.

Q. When should I pick honesty (Lunaria) *to dry the seedpods?*
A. Wait until the pods turn from green to brown. Gently rub to peel the brown outer skins off to reveal the papery cream-colored pods.

Q. Do you have any suggestions for controlling Chinese lantern from taking over the garden?
A. Try growing Chinese lantern in a container with drainage holes, above ground or sunk in the soil. Harvest the pods before they can self-sow.

Q. How do I keep the stems from breaking when I dry gomphrena?
A. Gomphrena stems are quite sturdy as a rule and do not require wire for added strength. Cut each stem as long as possible. Handle them with care, and hang them upside down to dry before using them in arrangements.

Write or call for a free Burpee catalog:
W. Atlee Burpee & Company
300 Park Avenue
Warminster, PA 18974
(215) 674-9633

SUGGESTED SOURCES OF SEED

DeGiorgi Seed Co.
1529 No. Saddle Creed Rd.
Omaha, NE 68104

Gurney's Seed and Nursery Co.
Yankton, SD 57079

Johnny's Selected Seeds
Foss Hill Rd.
Albion, ME 04910

McClure & Zimmerman
108 W. Winnebago
P.O. Box 368
Friesland, WI 53935
Excellent source of bulbs

Select Seeds
81 Stickney Hill Rd.
Union, CT 06076
Specializes in old-fashioned flowers suitable for drying

Stokes Seeds Inc.
Box 548
Buffalo, NY 14240

Thompson and Morgan
P.O. Box 1308
Jackson, NJ 08527

W. Atlee Burpee & Co.
300 Park Avenue
Warminster, PA 18974

THE USDA PLANT HARDINESS MAP OF NORTH AMERICA

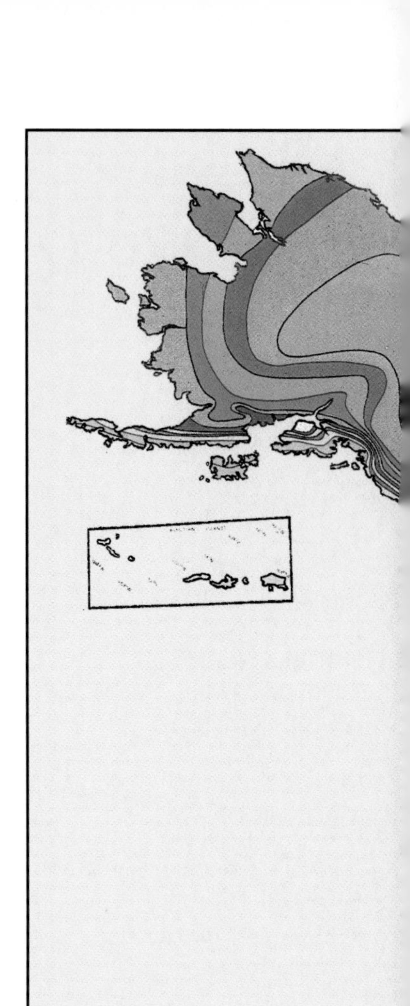

Average Annual Minimum Temperature

Temperature (°C)	Zone	Temperature (°F)
-45.6 and Below	1	Below -50
-45.8 to -45.5	2a	-45 to -50
-40.0 to -42.7	2b	-40 to -45
-37.3 to -40.0	3a	-35 to -40
-34.5 to -37.2	3b	-30 to -35
-31.7 to -34.4	4a	-25 to -30
-28.9 to -31.6	4b	-20 to -25
-26.2 to 28.8	5a	-15 to -20
-23.4 to -26.1	5b	-10 to -15
-20.6 to -23.3	6a	-5 to -10
-17.8 to -20.5	6b	0 to -5
-15.0 to -17.7	7a	5 to 0
-12.3 to -15.0	7b	10 to 5
-9.5 to -12.2	8a	15 to 10
-6.7 to -9.4	8b	20 to 15
-3.9 to -6.6	9a	25 to 20
-1.2 to -3.8	9b	30 to 25
1.6 to -1.1	10a	35 to 30
4.4 to 1.7	10b	40 to 35
4.5 and Above	11	40 and Above

This zone map provides a broad outline of various temperature zones in North America. However, every garden has its own microclimate.

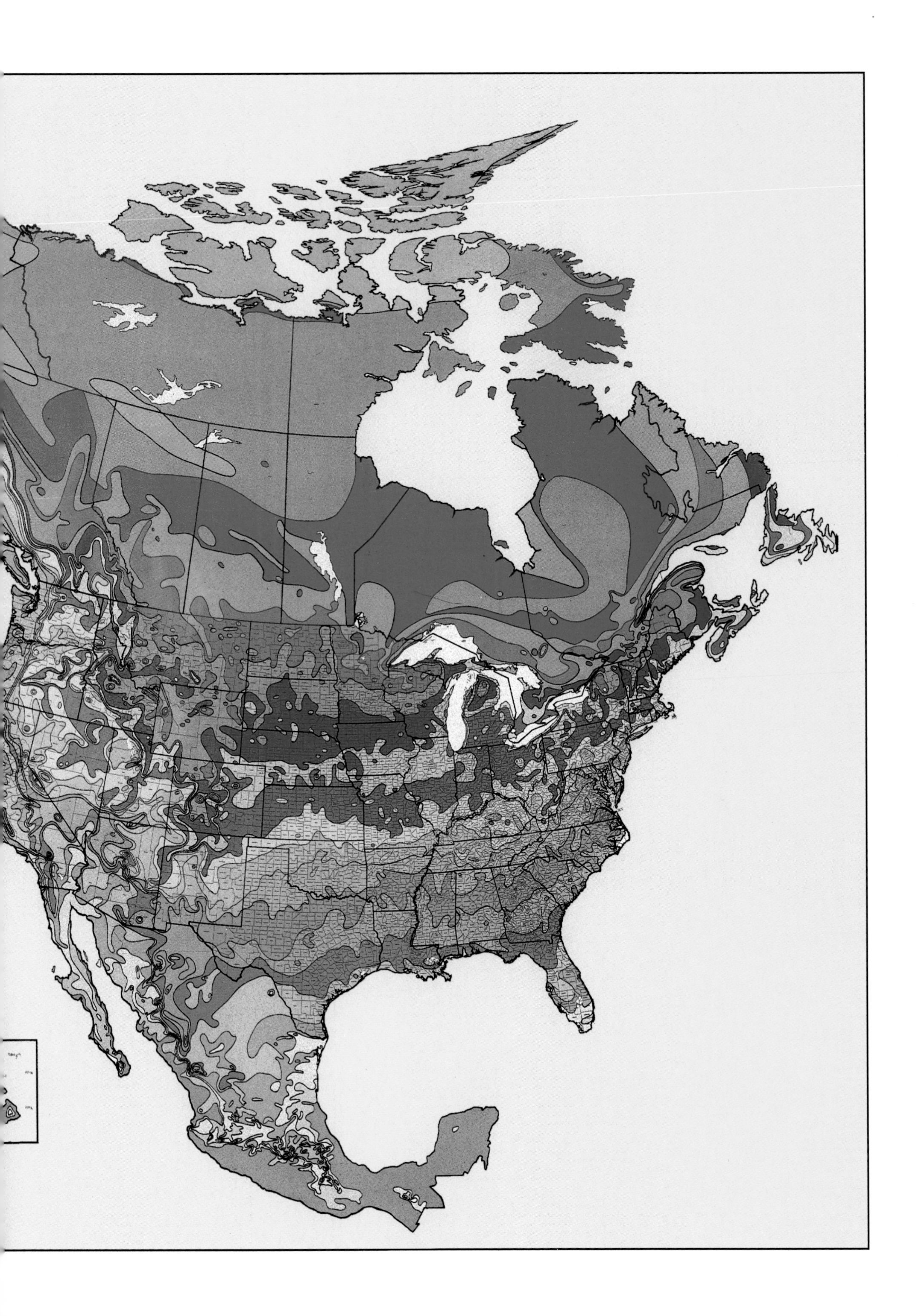

Index

Italicized page numbers refer to captions.